ENVIRONMENTAL TRACKING

Can Investment Revolution Prevent Ecological Catastrophe

Michael Gill

Pen Press
London

The LSE Drama Society

PRESENTS

'ENVIRONMENTAL TRACKING'

Can Investment Revolution
Prevent Ecological Catastrophe

A Global Stock Market Revolution
A Planetary EcoLogical Solution
A Global Stock Market Solution
A Planetary EcoLogical Revolution
A Global Stock Market Solution
A Planetary EcoLogical Revolution
A Global Stock Market Solution
A Planetary EcoLogical Revolution
A Global Stock Market Solution
A Planetary EcoLogical Revolution
A Global Stock Market Solution
A Planetary EcoLogical Revolution
A Global Stock Market Solution
A Planetary EcoLogical Revolution
A Global Stock Market Solution
A Planetary EcoLogical Revolution

Written and directed by Michael Gill

The Environmental Investment Organisation (EIO) Ltd is a non profit making organisation that has been formed by the Author to exploit ET (The Environmental Tracking Concept) for the benefit of the planet and its current and future inhabitants. No other organisation is authorised to utilise the concept without the EIOs prior permission.

First published unofficially by Carrots Anon 1994
An unofficial imprint of ROBIN HOOD ADVENTURES LTD

First published in Great Britain 1997

Pen Press
39-41 North Road
Islington
London N7 9DP

ISBN
1 900796 66 X

Printed and bound in the UK
on paper from sustainable forests

This work is dedicated to SamSon
and family; past, present and future.

About the Author

It is suggested that the following resume of the past is likely to prove about as relevant to the future as space travel.

The 'analyst' behind this drama was educated at The London School of Economics and specialised in such things as International Economic Policy and Nuclear Strategy. Unofficially, he specialised in drama productions and recently discovered that the combination of EcoMonics and Drama might make history.

Having pursued several different career paths before most recently working in the 'city' as an investment analyst and fund manager, the author, fed up with the stress and meaninglessness of making money for the sake of it, fell into a new position - *A self-funded eco-strategist (and humourist)*.

Qualifications for the job: as above. **Term of employment**: play it by ear. **Salary**: none in first three years, hopefully heading for a rise in the fourth. **Job Description**: solve the world's environmental crisis, without getting *too* serious about it. **First Task**: write a book about money.

FOREWORD
By
Herbert Giradet

Money as a tool for good? Impossible! Or maybe? With Michael
Gill I certainly agreed right away that "it will be very difficult to
solve anything if we cannot get money to work for us, rather than
against us."

Money is the secret agent of many of our actions. Yes, we all like
good value for our money, and high returns on our investments. But
as active or passive investors we may be unaware of our money
having appeared in the guise of saw mills cutting up mahogany trees
from fragile rainforests, herbicide factories with appalling
environmental records, or leaking oil wells in the North Sea. But
now, thanks to this book, we can see prospects for directing our
money to benefit the environment and to enhance the lives of future
generations.

Much of what defines our world stems from the power of money. All
technical innovations arise from the capital invested in them. But
money does not take responsibility for itself, and people rarely account
for its environmental impact. "The only possible route for persuading
money to start solving rather than causing the problem is to create
incentives for our economy and the people who work in it to serve
and respect the natural environment on which we all depend. Who
can fault that point? But where does it lead us?"

Well here we have a new tool in our hands: **Environmental Tracking.**
I agree with Michael that once applied to the full that it does have
real potential for getting the stock market, and therefore the economy,
to change its behaviour patterns.

In my own work as an environmentalist I have come to realise that we have tried to use many tools that turned out to be blunt and rather ineffective. For too long the environmental movement has tried to tinker with symptoms rather than homing in on the key role of capital in shaping our world. How it is invested is a decisive factor in what the shape of the future will be like. "We do not have a hope in hell of solving environmental crisis until we find a practical strategy for incorporating environmental priorities into the financial and economic system." I believe that here is a tool that could be as sharp as a samurai's sword, even if it is kept away in its sheath much of the time.

This is one of the rare books that conjures up a new world in the reader's mind, that opens secret doors that have been there all along if only we had seen them. Money as a tool for good? Well maybe yes after all. After reading Environmental Tracking it seems perfectly feasible to create new instruments for taming the power of money, or, to quote the author, "to reprogram the system that is causing the damage in the first place..." It is a book for investors, whether they want to invest in the planet or simply for themselves and their families.

This book will do its important job if enough people read it and tell each other about it. It is full of striking social invention. I like its idiosyncrasies as well as its deeply serious message. Let us make sure that it reaches the large influential readership it deserves.

Professor Herbert Giradet
Author and film maker
Chairman Schumacher Society
Global 500 Award Winner

CONTENTS OF THE DRAMA

The Prologue

ACT 1
If Money Is The Problem What Is The Answer?

Scene 1 - **The Power Of Money**

Scene 2 - **The Stock Markets Of The World - Red And Blue But Ultimately Green**

Scene 3 - **Why Specialist Green And Ethical Funds Do Not Work**

ACT 2
If Money Is The Answer What Is The Problem?

Scene 1 - **ET - A Business Plan For The PlanET**

Scene 2 - **ESP-The Environmental Scoring Panel**

Scene 3 - **What Are The Implications Of A Global ET?**

ACT 3
And Now For Something Completely Different.

Scene 1 - **The Humour Tracking Concept**

The Epilogue

The Prologue

Ladies and gentlemen. Since this book, or 'drama' as I have chosen to style it, is a proposal for the future, it is not possible to know now what its ultimate outcome will be. After all, history is littered with well intentioned ideas that have taken a very different course from the originators intention. However, whether this proposal becomes a global catalyst for unmatched positive change, or remains buried under the tidal wave of 'information overload' I believe we are drowning in, it is surely not for the author to prejudge the outcome.

So I have finally found the nerve to overcome the fear of failure and of the responsibility inherent in presenting this proposal to its audience. I take this risk knowing that, whatever the ultimate outcome, it could not possibly be anything worth anyone getting *too* excited about.

Having placed this work in some kind of perspective, what is its motivation? Very simple. It seems perfectly obvious that at this moment in our history human beings are presented with a blindingly obvious priority, and a very clear choice. Do we wish to preserve the conditions for healthy and enjoyable human life on this planet, both for ourselves and our future descendants? Or do we wish to pursue a course in relation to our environment which in the widest possible sense is utterly failing to meet that priority?

The situation compares to the well known story of Alexander the Great who was shown a knot that no one before him had been able to untie. The young Alexander briefly looked at the knot, then drew his sword and cut it in two. I hope to show that if we are prepared to boldly accept responsibility towards our environment as the cornerstone of our thinking, from which all other decisions and priorities flow, then the complex 'tragi comedy' of modern life can also be cut through like the Gordiaon Knot.

The purpose of this drama therefore is to present a logical, practical and marketable plan to exploit the immense power of the world's financial system to help solve our environmental problems, in a manner that almost everyone can participate in, and benefit from, and which I do not think any sane person could have any sane reason to oppose.

It might be useful to briefly consider how this situation came about in the first place How have the world's stock markets, which have only been in existence for some two hundred years - a mere spec in history - developed to a position where they now need to be harnessed to protect the environment from which our entire civilisation evolved over millions of years?

The conditions under which life on this planet emerged in the form of the simplest biological molecules, has been estimated by natural scientists to have begun at least 3000 million years ago. By the extraordinary process of 'chance' combinations of chemical compounds over millions of years, one particular compound, deoxyribo-nucleic acid, DNA, appeared and began the process by which life could reproduce itself in ever more complex forms, and in ever greater variety. As the 'imperfect' DNA copying process evolved slightly different versions of the same species were created as fish became monkeys, who came down from the trees and turned into us. Incredible but apparently true, give or take a few details that might benefit from further elaboration.

To use the scale of an annual calendar to pinpoint us in this process, the most primitive human beings emerged about half way through December thirty-first, got cleverer and cleverer in the course of the evening until with one minute left to midnight we worked out how to grow food while staying in one place. From this moment sprang civilisation, towns and cities, commerce and trade, art and science. The population sprang from ten million individuals across the entire planet to six billion in one minute. With two seconds till midnight the industrial revolution and the global financial system changed the human impact on the natural environment with greater speed than all previous generations put together. Ten years ago, a tenth of a second before midnight, as the juggernaut of development is accelerating across the globe, we begin to realise we risk undoing in a few remaining nano seconds what billions of years of evolution has created.

We have arrived at the here and now. On the verge of the year 2000. What is the fate of planet Earth in the 21st Century? Do humans seriously believe we can continue to treat this planet with the disrespect that characterises our industrial civilisation?

May I begin this self detonating acorn by asserting some basic premises that are **not** a matter of opinion.

i.　　The way our economies operate is a cause of great environmental damage.

ii.　　The economy needs to change the way it operates if we want to reduce that damage.

iii.　　No one is in a position to say how we might reduce that damage if they do not understand how an economy operates.

These are three irrefutable statements and anyone who is devoting energy to disagree with them is preventing the environmental crisis from being tackled and, ultimately, solved.

There is nothing complicated about what is proposed inside this drama; but for many, the effort required might involve no less than the overcoming of 'knee-jerk' reactions to issues they think they already understand. The unfortunate irony is that often it is some of the most 'educated' and 'expert' people who are most guilty of this 'knee-jerkism'. The most frightening thing about our current predicament is the utter mental laziness of so many who have set themselves up as 'opinion formers.' It can be found everywhere, across the entire political, media and environmental spectrum.

Has society become so absurdly complex that it cannot make rational choices? Have so many people become so absurdly 'specialist' that no-one can see 'the wood for the trees,' or 'the trees for the wood?' Is the result of knowing *so much* about one thing knowing too little about everything else? Where is the balance? Where is the common sense? (Buried under a mountain of 'information pollution', 'complexity' and 'expertise'?) Many people have become so 'pigeon-holed' they appear unable to question whether what they are doing actually makes any sense. Which is frightening. We appear to have evolved into a species of 'automatons'.

Many of those shouting loudest about their commitment to solving our planet's problems turn out to be the least open minded about what might actually be required to solve these. The 'expertise' or 'commitment' can become so specific and one sided that it can simply become another 'vested interest'. It becomes blind to perfectly *valid* propositions already dismissed as 'no go areas', without any further consideration. A mind that is not open to new possibilities cannot solve anything. We at the EIO trust that our audience are not such people. We trust we can agree that the plight of our planet needs a less prejudiced approach.

Beneath all the apparent complexity, the way our economy operates is very simple. As is what is proposed in this drama. But there is little possibility of the contents of this drama being understood by any member of our audience who is incapable of putting their preconceptions to one side; which, when it comes to questions of money and economics, is for most people very difficult. It is as if a body of thinking, comparable to the religious dogma of the medieval ages, has been allowed to develop in people's minds and in the media without it having any basis in reality. Yet the attachment to the thinking is so strong reality is 'presented' to fit.

When this book was first written in 1994 the Greenpeace slogan at the time seemed very logical. It read 'Whatever it takes'. Indeed. Unfortunately, I have never heard a convincing description from Greenpeace, or anyone else, of what it will take to reverse the disaster course we are set on. The reason for this, apart from the fact that we are attempting to solve the most complex problem human beings have ever been faced with, is I believe that nobody has attempted to answer the question from a truly practical standpoint. My starting point is this: it will be very difficult to solve anything if we cannot get money to work for us, rather than against us. The only possible route for persuading money to start solving, rather than causing the problem, is to create **incentives for our economy and the people who work in it to conserve and respect the natural environment on which we all depend.**

Now, many people may be surprised to hear that the fate of our planet depends on the stock market and understanding the subject of economics. However, I suggest that as clearly as night follows day, w*e do not have a hope in hell of solving the environmental crisis until we find a practical strategy for incorporating environmental priorities into the financial and economic system.* The environmental movement is too focused on the technology of solutions. There is no possibility of seeing these solutions transferred into everyday life unless we can create a structure that will incentivise those solutions. To do this we must look to the economic and financial system and understand how we can harness it. In the present system, **Solutions follow incentives**! That is the premise of this book. How could all that money, all that *power*, be **harnessed** to solve the world's environmental crisis?

It seems a perfectly reasonable question to ask. And the answer that presents itself appears perfectly **logical** and surprisingly **simple.** It also appears to be **practical.** It is called the **Environmental Tracking Concept.**

Having spent over three years trying to find the fault in its logic and after asking countless people to do the same I have finally concluded there is no fault in the logic of the **ET Concept.** Anyone else is welcome to find it but I suggest there comes a point in any debate where there can only be one true arbiter of whether an idea will work or not, and that is to put it into practice and see if it works!

So a book has been written about the idea. An initial structure capable of launching the innovation has been put in place; and one sincerely hopes the cavalry turns up!

As to why no one else has come up with the same idea, I can only conclude that no one else has asked the same questions from the standpoint which, by virtue of my particular experience and knowledge, I was able to take.

Who has this been written for? Well, is it too naive to say with all sincerity, everyone? Certainly, the audience for this drama will be very wide. It is for anyone who is concerned with the state of their immediate environment and that of the planet as a whole; who is prepared to accept that dealing with that challenge means dealing with the nuts and bolts of reprogramming the system that is causing the damage in the first place. It is a particular challenge to all those people involved in the 'environmental movement' and their millions of silent supporters to understand why we have got into this mess and how we might be able to escape from it. It is a passionate plea to stop making 'noise' that gets us very little very slowly and to start concentrating on the adaptation of the financial system which is needlessly perpetuating this tragedy.

It is also meant to be a young persons book. After all, the young are the future, and this book is very concerned with their future. I hope those working in education can use it to show students that idealism and conscience can find a practical route for expressing itself, even in this seemingly mad world. I hope that it gives the subjects of finance and economics a relevance and optimism that is not usually present in the standard texts dealing with these subjects.

It is, perhaps, ultimately a book for cynics and sceptics. After all, it has been written to satisfy the greatest sceptic I know; myself. This book and its ideas are a response to a deep rooted cynicism and scepticism, and if it can stand up to that, it ought to stand up to anyone's.

Finally, it is addressed to all those people who work in the investment world; perhaps the natural home for the world's arch sceptics. However, it is clear to me they are only doing what anyone who is an investor, be they a millionaire or an ordinary person paying into a pension or an endowment or any other kind of investment, is employing them to do with *their money. There is no point asking the investment community to undertake something that the majority of investors would not want to support with their own money since they are the beneficiaries who ultimately run the investment world.*

So this is a book for investors; whether they want to invest in the planet or simply for themselves and their families. It is a book that intends to square the circle and show how investing in the planet for the long term can also become the best investment in the short term; as a matter of survival. To achieve its purpose, it needs to be understood by anyone who has an investment in the stock market in any form whatsoever, which, when analysed, turns out to be the majority of the population in developed countries.

The presentation of this 'stock market drama for the planet' has been through many phases, in an attempt to balance two opposites: to be sufficiently credible and detailed for the 'experts', yet not so serious that it risks boring everybody else, who it is hoped might also want to read it. At least then the 'experts' will have a more informed audience to contend with when they come to pontificate in public on these urgent matters. The balance can be tricky at times, so if the going gets too heavy for your liking, do feel free to skip a few pages, and if it gets too light for your liking, well, try to *lighten up*. Don't forget -

'THIS IS EVERYONE'S ACORN'

ACT ONE
If Money Is The Problem What Is The Answer?

Scene 1
The Power of Money

Why does Money appear to get the blame for everything, by everyone? Radicals, socialists, environmentalists, new-agers, even right-wing reactionaries seem to blame it for the evils of the world.

To me, it's a bit like blaming politicians for everything. Who voted for them? We did.

We have voted for the world we've got. And we've been buying the world we've got. And now we're paying for the world we've got. The only snag is that it's not only us who are going to pay. The bills are only just coming in. Can we really expect our children to politely thank us when it is they who have to clear up this mess?

OK. Let's stop the guilt trip and come up with a 'gilt trip'. Let's think positive. 'Money talks'.
Can we change the script and give it something good to say? Yes, we can. If we are prepared to recognise that there is no mystery about how money operates. It is simply the <u>lubricant</u> *in a financial and economic system that can be understood, adapted and harnessed. If we are prepared to talk the 'language of money' and act with a boldness limited only by practicality.*

Money is, in fact, simply carrying out our instructions. The only reason the world is in the mess it is in is because we have chosen to use money to create such a situation. The reason the mess has become so big is because there is so much money carrying out so many instructions. Ten thousand billion dollars or thereabouts is an awful lot of energy to be used for better or for worse.

What is money and where did it all come from?

 Well, to answer that, we need to go back to our annual clock of the world's history; and five minutes to midnight, perhaps 35,000 thousand years ago. There was no money then, no stock markets, but people would trade by barter. A pot for an axe, or a supply of nuts perhaps? One thing we do known is that when human beings come into contact with other humans they begin to exchange items, partly as a means of turning fear and hostility into friendship and trust, and of course to better their worldly life. By the time settled communities had come into existence this bartering would have become so sophisticated and widespread that some more precise measure of what was being exchanged would have become necessary. For example, how could the farmer offer one bushel of wheat to the potter in exchange for one and a half pots? Perhaps the potter would find a smaller pot, or one very big pot; but what happens if the harvest is poor one year and the blacksmith is offering for that bushel of wheat a new plough, a new sword and some expensive ornaments? As soon as people start exchanging the fruits of their labour beyond their family, you have a market, and a market creates prices. Without a common measure for valuing each persons efforts, a recognised currency - in other words money -exchanges would be limited and imprecise.

Unfortunately, or fortunately, depending how you see it, human beings have been intelligent enough to develop more and more effective methods of producing an ever expanding range of goods, starting with the hunters who became farmers, who invented ploughs and growing techniques which meant they could grow enough to feed others who were now free to specialise in producing pots, paintings and practically anything else the human mind would conceive, which they all sold back to the farmer in exchange for the food they no longer needed to grow themselves because someone else had successfully worked out how to produce what previously had taken many. And so it went on. Sooner or later money had to come into existence to enable all these people who were specialising in more and more diverse activities, to trade with each other. The more these people produced, the more money came into existence. The fact that some accumulated a great deal more than others, and not all by fair means, does not make money itself in whatever form it takes, anything other than a sophisticated form of barter. Shopping in a supermarket is just a form of bartering for food in exchange for going to work everyday via the medium of a piece of paper the Bank of England prints, or a debit card somebody invented to save you time queuing at a 'hole in the wall'.

The problem now is that the scale of material, in terms of technological and human resources, that money can command has become so great that we risk destabilising the ecological system that evolved to support us.

Money has become mobile energy. *Every time* we spend (or save or invest) money, we set off a flow of consequences. It sends signals down the EcoNomic chain to produce whatever goods or services we have chosen. So when we spend (or invest or save) money, we are generating consequences. Consequences for us and our children who consume these things, for the people and the planet who produce them; and for future generations who will inherit the legacy of these choices. Think about it. Every time money is used, we are generating consequences as real as this world.

Money is obviously very powerful stuff. At the physical level it is surely the most potent energy on the planet. We use it to shape our physical environment - and for human beings life, whatever else it may be, is a physical experience. It is difficult to have a healthy and enjoyable life in an unhealthy environment. So hopefully there is nothing too controversial in stating that it is important to ensure that money is directed in a way that improves our health and environment.

We ALL have some of that power and every day we are ALL shaping the world and the environment we live in. Much of the world we experience every day has been shaped by the way money has been spent in the past. Since the industrial revolution the power of money to shape our environment has increased exponentially. Capital has been used to propel technology to a point where its effects are quite possibly approaching the point of no return. It is only as the scale of some of the consequences of these EcoNomic choices upon our environment become ever more apparent that more and more people are realising that money, and the technology it develops, cannot be used with indifference. To date, what we have in the world is the chaotic sum of the consequences of money. **When people become conscious of the consequences of the way they spend, or invest their money, the world can change for the better.**

It could take a long time; *indeed more time than we have,* for the majority of people to become environmentally *conscious* of the way they spend, and invest their money. And even if they did, not everyone can afford to buy conscientiously. So we need to come up with one or two practical solutions to the chaotic manner in which money is directed now.

Solutions are being suggested all the time. The problem is that they are trying to tame a GIANT to which they are just 'pin pricks'. To tame this giant we need to influence it in *exactly* the right place. In this analogy the giant is the **economic system** and if we *understand* how that system works we can pick the right spot to *tame* it.

There are thousands of worthy efforts being made all around the planet to deal with environmental damage. However, until we identify and solve the 'master problem' all that energy and effort will be wasted solving smaller problems, which are then easily *undone* again by the fundamental problem, in a very frustrating and futile loop. When you begin to solve the **cause** of the problem, all the smaller solutions can become much *easier* to implement and much more effective.

The **Environmental Tracking Concept** proposed in Act 2 is a stock market based solution that has the clear potential to get us well on our way to taming this giant, *very quickly*. How? By harnessing the immense power that is concentrated in the financial system enabling us to achieve desirable ecological objectives. 'The *Business Plan* for the planet' that can facilitate this adjustment does not require anyone's *permission* or any protracted *negotiations*. It only requires implementing. One single large stock market investor could get this ball rolling in a matter of months.

Presenting that stock market based solution is thus the main purpose of this drama. However, before embarking on that journey, I would like to outline a larger solution into which the **ET** innovation is designed to fit and which will be argued more substantially in a later instalment of this drama.

So first, let me outline what I, along with many others, consider to be the only fundamental practical solution to the environmental crisis and one of the intended *end results* of the innovation described in this drama.

Introducing 'EcoLogical Taxation'

In this opening scene I intend to outline why the ultimate solution, which is given different names by its various advocates, is **Environmental Pricing** and its logical implication, **EcoLogical Taxation.** It is, quite simply, a *'master answer.'*

An economy and every person and organisation in it, responds to prices and no other solution can ultimately work unless prices are encouraging people to adopt these solutions.

At the moment we have a system of incentives that actually discourages people from adopting environmentally beneficial solutions. A product, or service, which is produced or provided in a way that causes less environmental damage than a comparable product, is in the vast majority of cases more expensive to buy. That must rank as one of the most insane absurdities ever. Why? Because at the moment the environmental costs of different products are hidden from the consumer (be that a person or a company) to whom they appear to be free. However, the costs to the environment of any particular product or service are obviously very real and are going to be paid for in some form, at some time.

The 'Achilles heel' of conventional EcoNomics is its failure to price something (i.e. our environment) that has what I like to call **EcoMonic** Value and, like any scarce and valuable EcoMonic good, needs to be rationed. The 'free market' rations scarce and valuable things by raising their price. *Because our environment is not priced, because it is free, it is over-consumed and abused by producers and consumers alike.* Which on a planet of six billion people all wanting to drive cars, fly around the world, and enjoy a modern life style, is a recipe for global Armageddon.

'Exterminating Externalities'

In EcoNomics, students are taught about the concept of 'externalities'. This is the term used to describe the costs, and benefits, of a product or service which occur, but which are not included into the normal market price paid in the shops.

Having taught students this concept, EcoNomics then teaches students to forget this concept from their thinking and confine it to an obscure specialism. **EcoMonics** is the *same* subject except that it places these unaccounted for costs at the very forefront of its thinking. A simple difference that can change the face of the planet.

The entire environmental crisis is the result of companies and individuals consuming, and disposing of goods and services without having to incorporate the price of these 'externalities' into their decision-making. If pollution is free, why spend money trying to prevent it? If a car that pollutes less is *more* expensive than a car that pollutes more, what incentive is there to drive, or *invent,* a car that pollutes less? There is a reverse incentive! Is that logical?

'What does Environmental Pricing do?'

Environmental pricing, as anybody who is familiar with it will know, allows the 'free market price mechanism' to achieve environmental objectives. It can be implemented in many different forms in all sectors of the 'EcoMony'. Crucially, it can achieve those objectives whether or not the majority of people wake up and become environmentally conscious in their use of money. It is, in fact, the *only* fail-safe method of achieving this result because all the green consciousness in the world cannot enable an individual or an organisation to buy something he or she cannot afford.

What environmental pricing does is to ensure that the cheapest purchase available to the consumer is also the most environmentally sound purchase. A consumer or business can happily go about his or her business, buying the best *value for money*, and *automatically* making the best environmental choices.

'Cut the Hassle'

Why should someone enter a supermarket, which is stressful enough, and try to work out the impossible, namely, from a plethora of claims on a label, which purchase is the most environmentally friendly! How can a business manager, on top of the other responsibilities they might have, be able to work out which purchase causes the least environmental damage, when he can never have sufficient information or resources to do that anyway? Being alive is complicated enough without trying to work out the impossible. The simplest solution is to ensure that through an **EcoLogical Taxation Strategy** the best value for money is also the best environmental option. Then you don't have to persuade people to do things they cannot afford to do. They are automatically doing it because they cannot afford not to.

A Couple of Quick Examples

In everyday life, people often quote their own examples of goods and services that might be environmentally priced without realising what they are advocating. There are hundreds of examples. Here are a couple:

1. Consider organically farmed foods. Everybody says they would buy more of it if it was priced the same as food that is grown chemically assisted. Why isn't it the same price? One reason is because the environmental costs of intensive chemical farming, which has already exacted a tragic price on our countryside, and which we will all be paying for with hard cash at some point (in our water bills for starters), are not added on to chemically grown food at the point of sale.

Enter 'The Chickens that are Coming Home To Roost'

The cost of chemical farming and modern agricultural methods may be far more serious than we have even dared to imagine up till this point. To give one example, Christopher Booker recently wrote an article which was consigned to obscurity by the daily tidal wave of information. He mentioned a letter he had received from Professor Behan of Glasgow University, who is beginning to find links between ME and organo phosphorous chemicals and suggested that the ME problem could be the earliest indications of a long term epidemic. Anyone who knows anything about ME can grasp, as Christopher Booker put it, the horrific nature of this 'ticking time bomb'. It may well be that we have been literally poisoning ourselves and are only beginning to see the effects. 'Bon appetite!'

2. Consider a rechargeable battery. Why does it cost twice as much as a disposable battery? For the same absurd reason. The environmental costs of disposing of 100 unrechargeable batteries on 100 separate occasions are paid for in your taxes, which come out of your wage packet, instead of at the point of sale. When the toxic wastes from batteries, which are buried in landfills leak out, what do you think they eventually filter down to? Enjoy your drink!

Enter 'The Dreaded T-Word'

The word that normally causes the block on this concept is 'tax'. Under an EcoLogical Taxation System, taxes, in one form or another, are the means by which the full environmental costs of a product or service are added to the price the consumer pays. *The point that has not been fully grasped is that if you raise more tax in a way that reduces the consumption of environmentally damaging items, you need raise less tax from environmentally superior alternatives or existing sources of taxation, like your pay packet.* Not only could we end up being no worse off, we would be better off because we would have an environment that is actually more enjoyable to live in. If tax has to be raised anyway, why not raise it in a way that can help solve our most pressing planetary problems? If it makes so much sense, why is it not happening? It is called the 'wood for the trees syndrome'.

Turning an EcoLogical Taxation Programme into reality may not be easy. However, the speed at which once 'laughable' environmental solutions are being turned into government policy across the world is evidence of the human survival instinct waking up. Sooner or later environmental pricing will be in full swing. The only question is how much damage we want to see before we grasp the mantle and allow the 'invisible hand' of the price mechanism to deliver our 'EcoLogical Society', 'sustainable development' or whatever phrase you prefer to describe an environmentally healthier future.

The logic is inescapable. It is ultimately common sense. **EcoLogical Taxation** keeps presenting itself in any macro-economic solution as the keystone that has to be in place for every other solution to work properly. And the reason we are staking so much on this approach is because until we start implementing **ETax**, everybody's efforts in so many different fields are going to be constantly thwarted or undone.

Enter 'A Bird's Eye View'

The scale and complexity of implementing a comprehensive **Ecological Taxation Strategy** may appear frightening and there may be no easy route for arriving at that point. It will require no less than a 360 degree revolution in people's financial thinking. However, once our resistance to mastering the concept has been overcome, we will discover that we remain financially stationary; but environmentally considerably wealthier. In fact, because of the incentivising effect, created by switching taxation from people´'s income to their consumption, it is quite possible we may be better off both materially and environmentally.

Of course there are going to be initial objections, as can be seen everytime a Government makes limited efforts to implement it.   That is the point. **Limited efforts are doomed to fail.**   Citizens are far more likely to understand and accept an **ET**ax as part of a total solution to our environmental and economic needs if it is presented as such.

The key to its success is to give everyone a direct incentive in its adoption. I intend to demonstrate how the simplest and fairest incentive is to use the gradual adoption of an **ET**ax programme to fund parallel reductions in basic rates of income tax for everyone; and the provision of a universal basic benefit for everyone which would allow the complete scrapping of the social security system. To good to be true? No, I aim to show this trick is simple Rational EcoMonics!

However, this is not the time to expand on the detail of this strategy. I am simply wanting to flag the future direction in which the economy has to move towards if we intend to solve the problem. The purpose of the solution contained in this drama is to set up a dynamic within the financial system that will create the conditions for that fundamental solution to come into reality.

Exit 'Un-EcoMonic Industries'

Let us be absolutely clear about something that business and government have been telling all of us for years; namely that no one has the right to stay in an industry that is no longer economically viable. Or EcoMonically viable. Society, as they have quite rightly explained to us, cannot afford to subsidise something that is of little or no use to anybody. It would be cheaper to give people the money. Which is part of what I suggest.

But let us not hear this infantile argument that we cannot afford to lose an industry which is a net cost to society because its employees would be out of work. On that basis none of us would be doing the jobs we are doing now because we would all still be doing what our parents used to do. **When an EcoMonicaly unviable industry closes down, we do not lose wealth, we *free* resources (people, capital, raw materials) for use in a more *constructive* manner.**

This is exactly the process **ETax** would lead to. Industries that combine resources to produce environmentally damaging products and services need to give way to new industries that combine those same resources in environmentally constructive forms. Capital reforms itself; new jobs are created; and new tax revenues appear. It does not matter that some activities become unviable and others more viable. Capital is *mobile*. It would travel to wherever prices *signal* it can make a profit. Which is fine. **Profit simply motivates the ecomony to produce its wealth to a different set of priorities.**

We can still have a free market system where initiative and enterprise is rewarded. There would be some winners and losers in the process but the end result is not a decrease in ecomonic wealth. And there is one priceless reward at the end of this process - a healthier environment for us all to enjoy now and in the future.

Let us not be afraid of Environmental Pricing; a world where Environmental Pricing is in full swing could be a very exciting place to do business in, and a much healthier one.

The problem is that its logic is lost on many of the most powerful institutions in society. Such a radical reappraisal of what purpose the taxation system ought to serve is faced with major obstacles in the form of entrenched political thinking and business interests. It could take decades for such a consensus to emerge, or for the idea to gain enough public popularity to become a 'winner' for a political party to present to an electorate. We don't have that time. We need to find a mechanism which will attract enough financial backing to get the ball rolling now.

This is where our stock market based solution makes its appearance, and will make the key a lot easier to turn. Because business, instead of opposing this key, will be demanding it is turned. The only reason 'vested interests' oppose necessary environmental change is because they believe they are serving the interests of their shareholders. Fine. Our objective here is to create a mechanism where their biggest shareholders would be demanding an **Ecological Taxation Strategy** while simultaneously solving the problem at hand. Too good to be true? Save that conclusion until the end of this acorn!

'Money Talks'

Let us recap. Money has to be made part of the solution and anyone who thinks our problems can be solved by wishing money away is actually part of the problem. Money can be no more wished away than humans can be wished away. Money is nothing more than a liquid reflection of wealth, a means of exchange that comes into existence whenever two or more people wish to cooperate in work or trade. If it cannot be disinvented it needs to be harnessed. In the world today, very little can happen without money. So let us recognise this and make use of it.

Let us get the money talking green. Let us use the EcoMony to achieve some HarMony. Where do we start? What is the first move?

Introducing a 'Trojan Horse'

To succeed, our objective must have universal support. This way, its success makes everybody a winner. The objective we are working towards is the solution of the world's environmental crisis. Is anyone opposed to that?

Having determined our objective, we need an instrument that is as powerful as anything any opposition can deploy against it. Then we need to use it more skilfully.

The strategy advocated in this acorn is to use **all the money in the world**. It is difficult to argue with money. It is very persuasive.

Where can you find most of the money in the world? In the financial and stock markets. Who owns the stock market? You do. You and all the millions of other small investors paying their pensions, savings schemes and endowments every month. And several millionaires, whose role in our script we will be coming to.

To implement a successful strategy, it is necessary to do a bit of reconnaissance. We need to look carefully at how the stock market works and then devise an investment formula that makes more investment sense than any existing alternative. Then we can design *our* 'Trojan Horse' to enter the 'Citadel', without opposition.

Scene Change,

ACT ONE
Scene 2

Enter 'The Stock MarkETs Of The World'
- Red And Blue But Ultimately Green

The stock markets of the world act as the brain of the global economy! No wonder you might think, we are in such a mess.

If money is the energy that dominates this planet, the stock markets of the world are the world's power houses. Energy is directed on a truly huge and global scale. Because a stock market's function is akin to a financial brain, it is always anticipating the future. Capital follows a simple route - the route offering the highest return for the least risk. **Nothing will ever change that**. What we *can* change is the route which offers the highest risk/reward ratio.

Environmental pricing ought to eventually ensure that capital follows a route which leads all companies to pursue ever-higher environmental standards. Companies that fail to follow such a route will *decline* because the cards will be stacked against them. Those that excel in this approach are going to *thrive* because the cards will be stacked in their favour. *Capital can flow accordingly*. Now we are at the beginning of this process, of what I like to call an EcoMonic reshuffle from an EcoNomy to an EcoMony. There are very few safe investment propositions one can make but in this case it is a certain bet in which direction we are going. The environmental crisis is not some temporary fad. It is a fundamental challenge to the way we live which has to be resolved as a matter of survival. The result for the stock market is that green investing will become mainstream investing.

The day to day movement in share prices, that is mindlessly repeated every hour of every day throughout the financial world, is just the background 'noise' to the real influence of the stock market brain. Although some months are more important than others, like the crash in October 1987, when a hurricane arrived, but, in the great scheme of things, the daily and weekly movements are of little consequence. But this 'casino' image, from which some people earn notorious profits, is misleading. The financial markets are having real and important longer term consequences. **Everything you see around you is the result of capital being directed, via the financial markets, into concrete reality**. The stock market has arguably had a more revolutionary impact on people's lives, and our environment, than any political movement. However, the question now is, can we exploit the power of the financial system to create a positive revolution to favour not only us but also our environment?

Enter 'Green Business'

The environmental factor is already impinging more and more on business life, and companies are responding to this around the globe, not out of altruism, but self-interest. To the surprise of many, a commitment to the environment is turning out be good for business. Pressure is coming from consumers; from governments in the form of tightening legislation and early examples of environmental pricing; from businesses wanting to purchase from green suppliers; from insurance companies wanting to limit their liabilities; and last but not least from vigilant green pressure groups who have turned the media spotlight on companies' environmental records. The 'greener' companies are finding it easier to market environmentally friendly products; are able to anticipate legislation, rather than fighting a rear guard action to save misguided capital investments; are getting onto green supplier lists; are obtaining cheaper insurance; and are avoiding damaging publicity while receiving positive recognition for their efforts. Examples of green pressure on business could fill a book on its own, but our purpose is not to repeat what has been detailed elsewhere.

Why is it then, that the area where environmental pressure is lagging to date is the world's capital markets - the brain of the system? All those highly-paid brokers and the 'rocket scientists' who heap piles of reports on their desks every week that never get read, don't seem to be too interested. Are they, like those indifferent politicians, suffering from the 'wood for the trees' syndrome?

I intend to show that critical mass is waiting to happen but urgently needs a structure. The majority of investors would be happy to invest according to environmental criteria if a method could be devised that would **clearly benefit the environment** without any serious risk of **under-performing the main stock market index** on which everyone's performance is judged.

The professional investment community have not really grasped this yet, and none of the purportedly 'green' funds that do exist have, as I intend to demonstrate, been structured to take *advantage* of this opportunity.

If such a method could be devised, and was successfully marketed to the majority of investors, we would be making a quantum leap towards solving our problems. The brain of the economic system, the Stock Market, would actually be telling companies to do something intelligent!

It would be a global catalyst that could accelerate all those genuine, and up until now poorly appreciated, efforts that many in business are already taking to face up to the environmental challenge.

Money is very persuasive. Business can respond to its instructions rapidly because in the business and financial world, money is God. We can exploit the power of money to persuade business to play a leading role in solving our environmental problems.

People in business do not *want* to harm the environment. They are simply operating to an unavoidable commercial logic. If we take the trouble to understand how that system works, **we can help them change the system they are trapped in.**

The purpose of this scene is to lay the foundation for our proposal. We are going to explain what goes on in a stock market. We need to understand what drives share prices, and we need to clarify what risks investors are being exposed to when they place their assets into conventional 'managed' investment funds. The more clearly we can understand how the majority of money is invested at the moment, the more sense our proposal ought to make.

In the following scene, we need to examine why existing environmental funds, as currently structured, are not having any real effect on the problem.

Enter 'The Financial Cast List'

Who are the people that make up that euphemism, known as the 'City'?

They are all employees. They are employed by investors - you - to invest your money. Whether you have ten pounds invested every month or ten million pounds, they are simply there to provide a service and observe your instructions. Many people within the city and many outside seem to have forgotten this.

Who makes up the 'chain of command' in the city. Although there are literally thousands of specialities we can divide them broadly into 'thinkers' and 'doers'. The 'doers' are people who keep the wheels of this behemoth turning. They are the dealers who carry out buy and sell instructions in the market place. They are the brokers and salesmen who do some thinking, but mainly as a means of encouraging more deals, which is how they make their money. They are the administrators who tie up all the paperwork and legal 'ins and outs' of all this dealing. They are the financial advisors who sell the products of the behemoth to retail investors and, if they are independent, have to pass on other people's thinking about these products; or if not, pass on the thinking of the organisation which is also managing those products.

The 'thinkers' are people who try to work out how to get a better return on the money they have been given to invest by you. They are the fund managers deciding which companies and which markets offer the best value. In this they are assisted by the analysts, who usually study companies in a particular sector of the market, but some also broaden their horizons to look at an entire market, or markets, and the economy, or economies, that individual companies operate in. The analysts distribute their research in the hope that fund managers are persuaded to do their business through the analyst's firm, who charge broking commissions and dealing spreads. An unfortunate reality of this situation is that in their constant efforts to generate client interest for their employer, the analyst is prone to say something even if there is nothing to say. It is a rather silly and sad situation that only succeeds in generating an amazing quantity of written dross.

Enter 'Another Bird's Eye View'

There is one peculiar category of analyst who looks at the prospects of all the funds that are investing in these markets, and therefore needs to look at all the markets these fund managers invest in, as well as the different types of instruments the fund managers use. Although such an analyst cannot become an expert on each individual sector, he or she can gain a very good overview of how this behemoth functions, and quickly learns that all the sectors are operating to the same logic. It is a bird's eye view where one *can* see the wood for the trees. The person writing this acorn was such an analyst and this is his bird's eye view.

There is another peculiar category of thinker who is also a 'doer'. It is someone who invests their own money. Trading and investing other people's money is certainly very highly paid; but ultimately nothing terrible happens if you make mistakes. People investing their own money do not have that luxury. They have a peculiarly keen incentive to understand what is going on. It is highly likely that professional investment managers might try to take issue with what is said here because they are paid to be seen saying something that implies they are entitled to their salaries. And it doesn't actually matter whether what they are saying is true or not. They still get paid very high salaries. People investing their own money may be much more perturbed by what they read.

Back to the 'chain of command.' It always stems from the individual investor placing his money at risk via a financial advisor, a stock broker, direct with a Unit Trust Company, or through payments into a pension or insurance fund. Most actual investment is thus carried out by institutions who are employed by individual investors to manage their money, in unit and investment trusts, pension and insurance funds etc.

For every investor therefore, the issues have become: how successfully do institutions manage their money and how good is the manager?

I intend to show why this question, which so dominates the field of financial advice, is a cul-de-sac that obscures a more fundamental and pertinent issue, which is whether it is at all possible for the performance of any individual manager/fund to be reliably predicted? For a private investor looking at collective investment funds, what does the phrase 'past performance is not necessarily a guide to future performance', (which is repeated mindlessly by all involved) actually mean? It means two things that represent two distinct and separate risks for the investor.

'What Are The Risks Involved In A Stock Market?'

First, there is the **market risk**. Nobody knows what the market in general could do next. This applies to any market anywhere in the world. Because nobody is capable of predicting events or trends of the future with one hundred percent accuracy. The pattern of the last one hundred years may, or may not, be the pattern of the future. The general market risk exists for anyone with money invested in the stock market in any form.

Secondly, regardless of the general movements of the market, there is the **performance risk.** A fund that has in the past performed as well as, or better than the market in general, may no longer do so. Also there is the risk that the individual companies held in that fund might not perform as well as the market in general.

Each of these two separate risks are affected by very different factors; anyone who can grasp what these two separate risks are can understand what is going on in a stock market. Let us consider the first risk.

Enter Risk Number One - 'Market Risk'

A market's progression can never be in a straight line. Wherever it is going, it has to get there through a series of peaks and troughs.

The market risk is double-edged; there are short term risks and long term risks.

In the short term, you can never know for certain whether you are buying at the *bottom* of a trough or if it is still got a long way to go down. And you never know whether you are *selling* at the *top* of a peak, or if the party has only just begun. In addition, you never know whether the *long term* direction is up from a short term trough or down from a short term peak.

The long term direction is the most important prediction to get right because it can eventually supersede any error from short term predictions. Of course, all time periods are arbitrary; but for our purposes we are talking about the long term in years and decades, and the short term in months, days or hours.

The more a strategy depends upon short term predictions, the closer it is to gambling. The more a strategy concentrates on longer term predictions, the closer it is to investing.

We will concentrate on investing rather than on gambling. No matter how many man hours, brain cells and computers are employed, no-one can ever reliably predict short term market movements. Certainly, there are some people capable of getting it right more often than not, but there is no guarantee that on the occasion you give them *your* money their luck might not have run out.

Despite the voluminous quantities of daily and weekly comment concerning investment, it amounts to little more than noise, chatter and guesswork. Anybody who *knew* how to predict short term peaks and troughs would not be spending their time holed up in an office employed by you to guess them. They wouldn't need to. They would have retired on a yacht with more money than they could ever spend.

On the other hand, a long term investor can play it both ways. If investment decisions based on a long term perception of value prove profitable in the short term, a profit can be taken and the money invested wherever else the best long term value is identified. If the investment proves mis-timed in the short term, wait. If your original judgement was correct, your patience should be rewarded.

'What Drives A Stock MarkET?'

The first thing we should do is explain why company profits (earnings) determine share prices. Once this is grasped, the confusion of daily and weekly, even yearly, activity, can be seen in perspective. What follows may go into more detail than is ideal, or necessary for everyone. But please don't be put off by anything that seems over technical. This scene is basically a credibility exercise.

Many people have concluded that interest rates are the driving force of the stock market, because the short term ups and downs seemed to correlate with interest rate cycles. This judgement is misleading. Interest rates appear to have a dominant influence over the stock market because when interest rates change the stock market anticipates how this could alter the future availability of money for investment in the market. When rates are low, money is switched from no-risk interest-bearing investments, such as a bank and building society deposit accounts, to higher risk equities. This happens partly in anticipation of a future economic upswing, because the low interest rates are stimulating the economy; but also because the low interest rates have the effect of making the yield on equities seem more attractive than would be the case in a period of higher interest rates. This is exactly what has happened in most stock markets over the last three years. As the economy recovers and interest rates rise, all these incentives to invest in the stock market are reversed. It all sounds very convincing. None of this, however, contradicts the fundamental role that company profits (or earnings) play, over time, in determining the level of stock market prices in general; as well as the relative performance of individual companies within that general trend.

'Why Earnings Are King In The Stock MarkET'

A simple point can prove this. Let us say that between 1900 and today company profits or earnings grew on average by 0%, perhaps because, after all the booms and busts, average economic growth was zero over that period, or because any growth was distributed in higher wages or taxation rather than as profits. Obviously, within that average, some companies would have done spectacularly well, others spectacularly badly, but for the purposes of this simple example average company earnings would have been stagnant.

During this time interest rates could have experienced incredible shifts; up and down in response to the economic cycle. The stock market would have moved up and down with those interest rate cycles, but throughout nearly one hundred years the stock market would never have moved significantly beyond its original level because there was no earnings growth to support any upward movement in share prices.

Without wanting to become over technical, it is worth explaining that the only change in average share prices over those hundred years would have come from a change in the 'rating' given to those stagnant earnings. This is known as the Market Price Earnings (P/E) Ratio or Multiple, which could have gone up or down. The price earnings ratio expresses the size of a company's profits as a percentage of its share value. A price earnings ratio of ten means that the stock market value of a company is ten times the value of its profits. (Rather than getting too bogged down here, why not ask anyone offering financial advice or who you think is a knowledgeable investor to explain it. If they don't know, should they be advising you?)

The important point to note is that rises in share prices due to a higher P/E multiple are a speculative anticipation of future earnings and can easily be reversed. The P/E Ratio has recently been as high as twenty times earnings for the FTSE100 Index, which is historically high for the UK market. It has since been slipping. It is even higher in America. At the end of the day, speculative re-ratings of the market in general can only be sustained by real earnings growth, which can be quickly reversed if those earnings expectations fail to materialise. The classic modern example of a market where the PE Ratio was stretched by speculative buying to unsustainable levels was Japan which offers a salutary lesson on how long it can take a market to recover once reality dawns.

In practice, long term zero earnings growth would lead to a decline in the P/E ratio, and therefore share prices, no matter what interest rates were doing, because in such a market the only attraction would be the yield on equities, which would have to be considerably higher than any risk-free alternative interest-bearing security, (e.g.. a deposit account) to compensate for the extra risk. For the yield, which is based on the dividend paid out by the company, to become higher, the share price has to decline. (Again, if this seems unclear and you are interested, ask a financial advisor.)

The only reason the stock market yield is lower than risk free interest rates is because of the *expectation* of earnings growth. Yield is earnings dependent. If that prop ever looks like collapsing, ouch!

Hopefully, the logic is crystal clear and irrefutable. Earnings determine the long term direction and scale of stock market prices. Interest rates are only *clues* to the timing of peak and troughs on that earnings determined path.

'Back to Investment'

If earnings are the long term driving force of the stock market, then the general market risk for the investor is that:

1. earnings growth could cease or slow down in response to economic (or EcoLogical) trends.

2. the P/E rating given to earnings in general could decline. Although this swings with interest rates (low rates encourage higher P/Es and vice versa) it is also a speculative variable that can be governed by *fears* and *hopes* for the future. It is therefore a speculative extension of the first risk.

Thus, earnings have a double fundamental influence - the market responds to both their **actual** and **anticipated** growth.

Once a speculative swing takes hold, it can develop a momentum of its own and prices can become absurdly cheap or expensive before the long term logic of earnings reasserts itself.

When a market is crashing, over a period of days or months, it is a brave investor who decides it is cheap enough to buy. Likewise, when it is going to the moon, it is a very astute investor who decides it has gone too far. There is always some risk of being wrong in any market situation, and of losing some or most of your money.

These are the fundamental risks being taken with his or her savings by anybody with a Personal Equity Plan (PEP), a pension, life assurance policy or endowment, or any other type of stock market investment. So far those risks have been worth taking because the stock market index over the last 80 years or so, which is the longest period we have records for in the case of the UK, has benefited from sustained earnings growth and has out-performed any other form of saving, giving a total return in real terms (i.e. adjusted for inflation) of on average about 5% a year, including dividends.

Will it continue to do so? Well, as the regulatory warning says, 'past performance is not necessarily a guide to future performance'. History has longer time spans than eighty years to work with!

'Why Market Earnings Growth Is Not Guaranteed'

If the earnings growth that has propelled the market over the last hundred years is in fact unsustainable - if it has been based on the 'once in a life time' consumption of free goods - if it has in fact been purchased by 'mortgaging the future' - then there is no guarantee that earnings growth will continue to support current valuations.

In fact, it is, perfectly obvious that an extraordinary degree of adaptability is going to be necessary for the economy to continue providing the earnings growth that could enable stock market growth in general to continue. Of course, within that average there could be spectacular winners and losers who are already mapping out their futures. It should be, in the jargon, a 'stock pickers' paradise. Those with the clearest understanding of where this trend is leading are going to make the best predictions, and the best investment decisions.

This is where we detect shrewd investors becoming a little worried. They have just read something that they know makes sense and do not like what it implies. If a fundamental perception grows that the ecological crisis is going to put a *ceiling* on future earnings growth, the market is only going one way. This could be described as a 'ticking investment time bomb'.

What might detonate it? Or more to the point, trigger fears of it detonating? And what might be the nature of the fuse? No amount of technical analysis can answer that one. The trough we are talking about if this perception takes hold has no obvious bottom. So, we better get our thinking hats on. We need to create a framework, *quickly*, where companies can respond creatively to the inevitable need to solve the ecological crisis.

Enter Risk Number Two - 'The Performance Game'

Let us move to the second type of risk an investor takes. This being that the particular fund they have chosen, or more likely been 'advised' to choose, could under-perform the market index.

This is where the earnings logic comes into its own. Can your manager successfully predict which companies will offer the best earnings growth in relation to the current share price?

If they can, they have the equivalent of a tree that grows pound notes.

A company whose share price stands on a price earnings ratio in line with the average for the market, but whose earnings are consistently growing at, for example, double the market average, should eventually outperform, no matter what the market (or interest rates) are doing in general. If...

...anyone can successfully identify companies with these future earnings.

Any fund manager able to do that should *always* out-perform.

Predicting earnings growth is the 'holy grail' of the investment world. This is what anyone with a brain in the city is paid to do. Everybody else is just playing games and picking up lucky crumbs.

How does one predict earnings growth? With great difficulty. The further into the future one looks, the more difficult it becomes.

Anything can affect earnings growth. The common sense of the people involved in the company might top the list. Beyond that, the biggest influences are the expected growth in the market a company has for its products or services and the efficiency with which it can produce those products or services.

I happen to think that these two fundamental criteria for identifying earnings growth dovetail perfectly with the case for environmental investing. Of all the uncertainties that the prediction of future earnings faces, the least uncertain factor is that environmental pressures and opportunities for business will grow.

I also hold the opinion that the biggest general market risk could come from the ecological crisis that is brewing. We do not know what shocks and changes are in store, but we can be sure that once they arrive there can only be one outcome. There will be a heightening of all the environmental pressures on business on which we base our case.

Anyway, let us return to the discussion of the second type of risk an investor takes. If earnings rule the stock market in the long term, then unless a fund manager is able to predict earnings growth better than the majority of his or her colleagues, or is lucky, or has intuitive investment abilities, that fund will always, in the long term, under-perform the market.

This is the risk an investor takes every time he or she employs a fund manager to invest their money.

Enter 'A Zero Sum Game'

What is not widely appreciated is that out-performance can only be achieved at the expense of someone else's under-performance. It is a zero sum game. It is, in fact, impossible for the majority of professionally managed funds to out-perform the index against which their fund competes. A manager who sells shares that he correctly believes will under-perform the index needs to sell them to a manager who will, by definition, then own shares that under-perform. Likewise, any shares that a manager buys, which out-perform, will have been sold by a manager who must end up *under*-performing.

By definition, they cannot all be buying shares that outperform and sell ones that under perform. At the end of this process, all the research, dealing, administration, marketing and commission costs ensure that the average performance of managed funds has to be lower than the index. It's an expensive merry-go-round which the *average* investor foots the bill for.

This is a simple truth that cannot be contradicted.

This is why the stock market is, in essence, a parasitic mechanism. It cannot create the earnings growth which we have seen is the basis of the benefit to the investor. It simply consumes a significant portion of the benefit to investors of that growth because all its players are competing against each other for the same cake. Ouch!

Does this mean that we don't need a stock market?

Of course not. Although investors could be better off with a simpler mechanism for allocating capital that does not *waste* huge amounts of resources, time and human talent that could be spent more productively.

'How Can You Avoid A Fund That Under-performs?'

You cannot. The standard warning, "Past performance is not necessarily a guide to future performance" is even more true of this second risk than the first general market risk.

Lucky managers, overseeing funds that *out*-perform, may be head-hunted by an unlucky investment firm that has *under*-performing funds. Their replacement may be one of those unlucky managers. A manager with 'good intuition' who, up until now has had a very good track record, might be experiencing difficulties in his personal life, and not able to concentrate on his work so well. Or the 'formula' that enabled a manager in the past to identify good earnings potential may just stop working, because times change and there are a whole host of variables that cannot be consistently predicted.

There is no single reason or consistent method that can predict a managers out- or under-performance. Which is why top slots and bottom slots in the performance tables are always changing. Some groups come out better overall, to be sure, but we all know that "there are lies, damned lies and statistics". Whatever a management group may demonstrate about the past performance of its funds, it can only out-perform at someone else's expense, and since everyone is chasing the same grail, the risk is ever present that one of its rivals can come up with a better combination of luck, intuition and prediction and send it further down the performance tables.

Which means that, unless you are incredibly well informed about exactly who is managing a fund, how he or she operates, whether his or her family is suffering because of all their hard work, and how long they might be going to stay in that position, looking at past performance figures is not too far away from being a complete waste of time.

I regularly spoke to the managers of these funds, and produced research on the performance of their funds. I soon realised these performance arguments were a complete farce. One could prove almost anything by choosing different periods of time for comparison; but, more fundamentally, because no performance statistics could actually prove anything because all the variables that might have explained those differences were unrepeatable!

All the marketing campaigns in the world cannot refute the simple truth being pointed out here.

Any 'managed fund' creates an extra risk for the investor, and no record of past performance can eliminate that extra risk or prove anything about the future. There is nothing else worth adding about the Performance Game, so we'll continue setting the stage for the real drama.

A Recap On 'The Scene So Far'

1. The short term direction of a market cannot be consistently predicted by anybody. If they could, why would they tell *you*?

2. The only long term determinant of share prices is company earnings. Nobody can reliably guarantee their future direction either, or a one-off change in 'sentiment' or real interest rates which could alter the market P/E rating.

3. The only sensible investment advice is that which makes a thorough relative assessment of the prospects of all the available investment options. Yet the wider the investment field you are being advised on, the more *superficial* the advice will inevitably be.

4. The people managing the funds you are being advised to buy face the same problem. The more comprehensive their review of investment options, the more superficial their assessments will be.

It is hard enough attempting to predict all the variables involved in one company. The variables are magnified if the prediction is being made for a fund that invests throughout the domestic market. Risk is spread, but so is the quality of the advice. Once the advice starts to cover Europe, America, Japan, The Far East, Latin American and every other emerging market that exists, we enter Mickey Mouse territory. Yet you can read such 'advice' every weekend in the financial pages, and you hear quite a lot of it in the City.

Once you add all these variables to those which affect the performance of a particular fund manager, then we are on a different planet. **The entire edifice of investment advice is, simply, a joke.**

'Where Does This Leave The Investor?'

Once an investor commits money in whatever form to the stock market, they are accepting the general market risk. From this point, three choices exist:

1.   Try to out-perform the market using your own combination of luck, intuition and predictive research.

2.   Employ a fund manger to do it - of whom at least in excess of 51% of them will under-perform the main market index, as explained, by a completely unpredictable degree.

3.   Buy into an index fund which simply aims to replicate the general market index without making any attempt to outperform; and thus avoiding any risk of under-performing.

Index funds will be explained in further detail during Act 2. In effect, a long term investor in an index fund is abandoning any attempt to out-perform the market, and has simply accepted the performance of the index itself as the safest risk reward investment path. In terms of earnings, index investment is simply relying on the *average earnings* growth of the market rather than attempting to predict which companies will have the highest earnings.

It seems obvious to me that of the risk/reward choices outlined so far, investing in an index fund wins hands down because it simply recognises that any method which seeks to out-perform exposes the investor to the risk of under-performing.   Index Funds are being recognised more and more widely as a valid method of investing and I expect the future to be dominated by index funds as this merry-go-round of managed fund guesswork and meaningless performance statistics is recognised for what it is: Information pollution 'par excellence' and a colossal waste of everybody's time and money.

'Where Does All This Fit In With The Environment?'

So you survived all that! Well done. Things get easier from now on.

As suggested earlier the majority of investors would be happy to invest according to environmental criteria **if** a method could be devised that would clearly **benefit** the environment; and yet avoid the risk of *under*-performing the main stock market index on which everyone's performance is judged.

The purpose of Act 2 is to demonstrate how such a fund with an environmental purpose can be designed to achieve this, and be capable of being launched on a very large scale, very quickly.

That is where we are going to leave behind what is wrong with the present system and propose a positive innovation that can have a major impact on the workings of the financial markets - **in favour of the environment**. But we need to lay out one final piece of groundwork. We need to tackle another set of myths; that is to understand why the current structure of green and ethical funds prevents them from having any fundamental effect on the financial system. We must ensure that the foundations of this acorn are absolutely **ROCK SOLID**.

ACT ONE
Scene3

'Why Specialist Green and Ethical Funds Do Not Work'

In this scene we are going to make some observations about the current crop of 'green' and 'ethical' funds that some people may take exception to. However it should be noted that what follows is an attempt to be constructive and is not meant to be taken *personally* by anyone. We are simply interested in finding the most effective solutions.

I intend to demonstrate why green investing, as currently understood and practised, is a flawed concept, because of how they are structured. They will always remain small players, niche funds exerting no real *power* over the stock market as a whole.

While existing approaches to green and ethical investment can be seen as a crucial *first* step - an education, a building block, but the time has come for them to move on to bigger things and reward previous efforts with a solution that potentially *could change the face* of the planet.

We have, in fact, come to the conclusion that these specialist green funds are trying to sell something to the green investor that does not exist. The objective itself is probably *unique* in human history by the degree of *consensus* it attracts, creating an *amazing opportunity,* which green funds, as currently structured, simply cannot capitalise on.

Enter 'Confusion'

The first problem is one of confusion of terms. 'Green Investment' continually gets mixed up with 'Ethical Investment', which is a much wider and vaguer concept.

Green Investment is a response to an objective environmental crisis that industrial society has produced. The majority of the population would agree that this crisis is undesirable and requires action. 'Ethical Investment', on the other hand, is a response to a much *wider* range of more *subjective* issues. Frankly, the number of issues which could be included under the banner 'ethical' are so contentiously diverse that an utterly meaningless concept called 'Ethical Investment' is the result.

It is ludicrous to imagine that a fund manager can:

a) know all the ethical preferences of his or her individual investors;
b) identify and eliminate/select all companies that contradict/support those preferences; and
c) convert these factors into a coherent investment strategy and state it is having the desired effect.

Who can say in any given set of circumstances what is ethical?

The arms trade is a favourite target of ethical investment. Has it been ethical at any point for a company to supply arms to the Bosnian Muslim Army, or Rwandan Refugees or any other persecuted minority. Was fighting the Gulf War Unethical? Was not supplying arms to the inhabitants of Southern Iraq ethical? In any situation where defenceless civilians are being massacred, is supplying arms for their protection ethical? We don't know. Who does? How can fund managers make judgements as difficult and personal as that on behalf of all their investors. Let's face it, it's a superficial guilt trip.

But I have no wish to get bogged down in the rights and wrongs of ethical investment funds, which is not the issue here. We simply wish to clarify that they involve making judgements on a *much wider range of issues* with a degree of *subjectivity* which makes them quite different from a fund designed to raise environmental standards, which is a universally recognised necessity.

So are the current range of green funds having any great success in achieving that objective? The unequivocal answer must be **No**. Let us consider why not.

Enter 'The First Flaw'

Attempting to 'select' those companies sufficiently environmentally minded to be included in a green fund is a near impossible task. No company is completely 'green' or 'ungreen'; it is a matter of *degree* requiring a very *comprehensive* assessment, rather than absolute judgements. Making such simplistic and arbitary judgements borders on the absurb and risks a mockery of the integrity of the green investment concept.

From a practical point of view for a manager running a normal fund, establishing which companies are sound investments is a full time job in itself. A green fund has to divide its research time between *two* full time tasks: a company's financial/business prospects and its environmental performance. Inevitably, the effort 'falls between two stalls.' When you consider the tiny size of many of the green funds; the number of potential companies for research on both these criteria, *and* then the fact that they may have only one manager and an assistant - if they are lucky - one begins to see the impossibility of any **serious** green investment assessment.

This assessment procedure is completely *unstandardised* between different funds; in some cases virtually non-existent, or based ultimately on little more than a manager's personal whim. The goal posts are always moving. Today's 'green technology' can be quickly discredited by a *new* invention or idea. Supporting so-called 'end of pipe' pollution technologies may, in fact, be undermining more fundamental 'clean technology' solutions. This sort of dilemma is *inevitable* when green money is trying to support particular solutions rather than trying to encourage the search for the **right** solutions.

An example of this superficiality was highlighted by an investment switch between two supermarket groups by one of the more highly rated green funds. The switch was based upon the difference between the stated 'green field sites policy' of the two groups in their out of town building programme. For an investment switch to be made on the basis of apparently this one issue is pure 'mickey mouse.' There is an inevitable superficiality that results from trying to make single issue either/or judgements about companies for the purposes of green investment. Large companies will inevitably demonstrate a range of plus or minus factors in any environmental assessment. Anyone taking a serious look at the portfolios of the existing green funds might find as many logics as there are managers to the content of these portfolios.

The solution we will come to in the next Act is not to make absolute either/or decisions about a companies green performance.

Enter 'The Second Flaw'

What is the second consequence to follow from trying to 'select' 'green' companies? The choice for the green fund is severely limited. The more fundamental the 'green' criteria, the fewer the possible investments. Some sectors may have no suitable companies and, inevitably, the fund bears little resemblance to the main stock market index. As it happens, this has not harmed the performance of most green funds, as many of the smaller companies in their portfolios have out-performed handsomely.

However, as every investor keeps being reminded, 'past performance is no guide to the future'. New, competing environmental technologies can quickly emerge, and small specialised companies trying to sell a particular solution are not sure bets. For a whole host of reasons there will be winners and losers even in the environmental field. Which is fine for those investors happy to live with that risk. They can keep investing in the 'green specialists.'

Most investors, however, do not invest in funds which avoid the majority of the largest companies. These companies, who, in the case of the UK stock market, account for near on 75% of the market's capitalisation, by definition provide the risk profile the majority of investors are *prepared* to accept.

Enter 'The Third Flaw'

This leads to the third reason why green funds as currently structured will always remain niche players; because even if this perceived riskier profile did not exist, the green funds, as currently constituted, could not handle really significant sums of green money. *There would be nowhere for it to go.*

If there are only a limited number of so-called 'pure green plays' on the stock market, consisting mainly of pollution control specialists and a few recyclers, who crop up in all the portfolios of green funds, any really serious influx of money invested under current criteria would send the shares of these companies rocketing. Anybody with any sense would then sell them at super profits.

Is this the purpose of green investing? To send a few specialist shares rocketing to unsustainable prices at which others cash in? Of course that would be no one's intention, but that is the corner green fund managers would be boxed into, given current criteria. The more successful Green Investment Funds are at persuading people to invest in them as currently conceived, the more absurd this outcome will be. Green investment cannot come to dominate the stock market until a criteria is developed which can be applied to the largest companies in the market. In fact, the current structure of 'Green Funds' *prevents* the majority of investors from supporting environmental objectives. Which is truly absurd!

Enter 'The Fourth Flaw'

This leads to the fourth objection, which involves asking: what is green investing trying to achieve? The answer seems clear. It is to use the position as a *shareholder* to *encourage* higher environmental standards amongst companies. Companies have to do what their shareholders demand. When the majority of those shareholders are saying 'go green', they will have no choice but to implement such a policy.

So the question is, how to structure an environmental fund that would appeal to the majority of investors? And in so doing, create a pressure throughout the EcoMony to raise standards. Is it, in fact, political investing, as it is clearly trying to serve a purpose beyond making money? The answer must be yes, but it is failing because the current structure of green investment is missing most of the market.

If green investment, as currently understood, had any chance of succeeding in changing the EcoNomy into an EcoMony, one could try and work around the first three objections. But how can the green funds achieve that when they exclude the majority of companies in the market? **If they have no relationship with those companies who most need green pressure, how can they hope to influence them?**

The result at the moment is that green money is directed into a narrow group of shares, on a spurious selection procedure, whose prices would, with any serious influx of money, become absurdly inflated against the rest of the market, without any real pressure being exerted on the market as a whole. So what's the point? There isn't any, apart from cashing in on specialist green 'success stories'.

Superficial guilt trips are not going to solve anything.

To have the nerve to make such damning criticisms, you may be wondering what is going to be suggested that could avoid those criticisms. But before doing so, I would like to reiterate that these criticisms are not levelled at any of the managers themselves. They are obliged to operate as best they can under the concept of green investing as it has evolved to date. I am sure that most of them would be the first to welcome any mechanism that could overcome these limitations.

Exit 'Specialist Green Funds'

Before the real drama begins, which we thank you for patiently waiting for, let us summarise what would be required for a new type of green fund to really **Take Off.**

We need a proposition that nobody in their right mind could refuse.

1. This new investment vehicle would have to be structured in such a manner that its research time and resources could be fully directed towards the environmental assessment of companies. It would not be getting involved in a dual financial and business assessment. This would enable it to do its environmental assessment properly but still have reasonable management costs.

2. The fund would have to invest according to a comprehensive and transparent green criteria that was vetted by an authoritative independent panel of experts that **included green pressure groups.**

3. It has to be invested in a manner that could absorb an unlimited weight of money, which can only be a blue chip fund based on the largest companies.

4. The fund would have to operate in a way which created a pressure on all companies in the market to improve their environmental performance.

5. The fund would have to demonstrate an investment case that offered the prospect, over time, of some degree of out-performance of its competitor funds.

6. It would require a fund whose risk profile was very similar to the current risk profile of the majority of invested money. By definition, the way the majority of money is currently invested represents the level of risk those investors are prepared to take. For a green fund to attract the majority of those investors, it has to be a blue chip fund based on the largest companies.

7. The formula would have to be capable of being replicated **throughout the stock markets of the world.**

A Stock Market fund that could meet such a criteria would put green investing, and the planetary environmental benefits that could follow, **in very serious business**.

ACT TWO
If Money Is The Answer What Is The Problem?

Scene 1
A Business Plan For The PlanET

Enter An Alien - 'ET'

The Environmental Tracking Concept, ET for short, describes a new investment method which is designed to appeal to a sufficiently large pool of investors to fundamentally alter the impact the stock market exercises upon the environment.

ET combines two existing but hitherto separate investment approaches; conventional *index tracking* and *environmental* investment, into one low risk but powerful green investment method.

The **Environmental Tracking Concept** begins with all companies in the relevant index in the same way as a conventional index fund but then *reweights* them according to a detailed *environmental ranking* carried out by a broadly based **Environmental Scoring Panel** (**ESP**), which is then published as the **ESP Ranking**.

I hope to demonstrate how this simple investment innovation, the creation of an *Environmental Index* paralleling the Conventional Index, can have a radical effect in financial markets. This hybrid goes beyond any existing green investment approach by applying environmental criteria uniformly across the whole range of companies listed on the stock market and, through the **ESP Ranking,** applies a *direct* pressure on each company to bring environmental concerns to the forefront of their business activities.

Enter 'Carrots And Sticks'

The pressure exerted on companies would be of the carrot and stick variety. It would reward companies for raising standards and penalises them for not doing so. Rewarding someone is always more effective than criticising them. Carrots taste better than sticks!

The investment half of the concept is based on the adaptation of conventional tracker or index funds first noted in Scene 2. This approach to investment management is known as 'indexation'.

These funds are exact replicas of the relevant stock market index (i.e. no manager is actually making decisions) and have been developed because it has been demonstrated, through published performance statistics, that the majority of non-index funds, over a period of time, cannot match the relevant index, for all the reasons explained in Scene 2.

As previously demonstrated, it is, in fact, impossible for the majority of professionally managed funds to out-perform the index. A manager who sells shares that he correctly believes will under-perform the index must sell them to a manager who will, by definition, own shares that under-perform. Likewise, any shares he or she buys that out-perform will have been sold by a manager who will end up under-performing. At the end of this process all the research, dealing, administration and marketing costs ensure that the *average* performance of managed funds must be *lower* than the index. It's an expensive merry-go-round which 'muggins' - the average investor - you, foots the bill for.

Index investing is one step above the 'dart board' theory of investment where it has been shown that random throwing of darts at the financial pages can produce a portfolio which can equal or out-perform a 'professionally' managed fund. By simply replicating the index, an investor eliminates the risk which will *always* exist with any managed fund of under-performing the index, in some cases quite severely.

Because index funds are all computerised and have no *research* costs they have much lower management expenses. Over a period of time this can have a significant impact on the return to the investor.

An 'ET' Based On The FTSE100

The effect of the environmental ranking that **ET** would use is, to use the case of the FTSE100 as an example, to reward the 50 companies with the highest overall environmental score with a larger purchase of their shares than would be the case if the fund was strictly replicating the index. Similarly the 50 companies with the lowest overall environmental score would be penalised with a smaller purchase of their shares than would be the case if the fund was strictly replicating the index.

This simple innovation which has been staring us all in the face can, if fully exploited, have the most profound environmental effect.

The degree of re-weighting (i.e. by what factor companies were under or overweighted) would determine how far **ET** diverged from the actual index.

Such re-weighting would be progressive. For example, if we set the maximum re-weighting at 50% for the two companies at the top and bottom of the environmental ranking, and descended to zero for the company in the middle, this would give a mean re-weighting across the index of 25%.

As an example, if The Body Shop was given the highest environmental score in the rankings, its weighting would be increased by 50% in **ET** compared with a conventional tracker. If British Telecom was ranked second, its weighting would be increased by 49%. And so on. At the other end of the rankings the effect would be mirrored with under weightings compared to the conventional index. The point to note is that although the re-weightings look quite dramatic at the top and bottom, for the majority of companies in the middle the weightings for **ET** would be very similar to the conventional index.

(The exact variance from the index which the re-weighting would cause is a technical point which would depend on whether the market capitalisation of the companies at the top and bottom of the environmental ranking represented a similar distribution to that found in the conventional index. There is no reason to assume that the size distribution would be very different between the two indexes. If the companies at the top and the bottom, where the re-weightings were highest, were the smallest companies in the index, the actual divergence would be less than 25% and vice versa.)

The result is a fund whose risk profile is very similar to the FTSE100. Yet this fund is able to perform its vital environmental mission by creating a pressure and an incentive for all companies to climb up the rankings.

Enter 'A Cake You Can Have And Eat'

Because **ET** will be weighted towards the most environmentally conscious companies, it stands to gain from any out-performance those companies achieve in a world of ever-increasing environmental standards. It seems logical to conclude that the ever-growing pressures on business, in the form of legislation, taxes, penalties, customer and supplier preferences, will, over time, affect the earnings of all companies.

We have already seen how earnings are the ultimate determinant of share prices. Companies with the highest earnings growth will ultimately see their share price out-perform their competitors. This is the basics of any stock market and, over a period of time, nothing can contradict this principle.

In this new business environment, one would expect some companies to be more successful than the average and **ET**, without taking any aggressive investment views, is likely to benefit from this to a greater degree than the conventional index.

It really is a case of having your cake and eating it!

'How ET Creates A Competitive Environmental Pressure'

An **Environmental Tracker** will create a competitive pressure upon every company in the index to improve its environmental performance. This effect occurs at several levels:

Enter 'The Spotlight Effect'

The Environmental Scoring Panel will be scoring companies annually using a transparent and widely-canvassed 10 point criteria. Companies in the index shall be ranked from 1 to 100.

No company would wish to be identified as having the worst environmental performance in the FTSE100. Nor could any company afford to relax its commitment if it wants to avoid that spot. This alone would be a serious commercial pressure, and the effect of the fund would be to make that pressure felt by all companies.

On the other hand, being scored top would be a very valuable carrot to beat your competitors with, as well as to dangle in front of your customers.

Enter 'The Share Price Effect'

The effect of **ET** would be to reward those companies with the highest overall environmental score with a larger purchase of their shares than would be the case if the fund was strictly replicating the index. This share price, being the sum of total supply and demand, would have to achieve a higher price than would otherwise be the case.

This not only rewards management directly in its prime assumed role of serving shareholders but sends a more important general market signal. It gives companies with the highest environmental standards a higher rating (Price/Earnings ratio) than would otherwise be the case and makes capital *cheaper* for them to raise than those companies at the bottom of **ET's** corporate environmental ranking. The bigger **ET** becomes, the larger the effect; its impact and future quite literally the biggest thing since sliced bread!

The stock market is a rationing mechanism for distributing capital. That is its function. To date it has done so without any environmental criteria affecting that process. It's about time that changed, don't you think? The ultimate effect here is to direct capital towards those companies with an environmental conscience and away from those without. It is, in fact, a form of environmental pricing.

ET is anticipating the way the EcoMony will have to react to the environmental crisis and is pricing capital accordingly. Clever, eh?

Enter 'The Dialogue Effect'

The Environmental Scoring Panel, on behalf of **ET** will, as a legitimate shareholder, be encouraging and systematically approaching all companies within the index to assess their performance against the established scoring criteria. Although many companies are giving a higher priority to environmental issues this will encourage *every* company to focus on how their business can be greened.

What if some companies do not co-operate with the work of the scoring panel? Well, some of the information required for the scoring criteria (which we are coming to) is already publicly available and the panel will have to work with the information it has been given. A company cannot complain if they find themselves ranked near or at the bottom of the rankings and find their business and share price suffer accordingly because they did not respond to the panel's request for information. Touché.

ET versus 'Existing Green Funds'

It ought to be immediately apparent that the **ET** concept is approaching the subject of environmental investment from a completely different starting point compared to existing green and ethical funds and has been specifically designed to avoid their limitations discussed in the last scene. Instead of trying to pick individual stocks that are deemed to be producing supposedly 'greener' products or services than other companies, the fund includes all stocks and *ranks* them environmentally. It then designs a structure that although linked to the index creates a pressure throughout the market to raise standards. This is, on the one hand, a safer approach from an investment point of view and at the same time more overtly political in the spirit in which 'green investment' was always supposed to be, i.e. as a force acting in financial markets to make *all* companies improve their environmental performance.

Enter 'Another Cake That You Can Have And Eat'

ET could be structured so that a percentage of assets under management, say 0.25%, could be channelled into the **Green Ventures Fund** while still being retained as the investment of the investor.

Each year an investor in an **ET** type fund invests 0.25% of his investment in the Green Venture Fund. Each year his holding in that fund increases. Of course there is nothing to stop **ET** investors from investing more in the **Green Venture Fund,** if they chose to. Holdings in the **Green Venture Fund** would be a separate share holding to **ET** holdings and could be sold at any time.

The beauty of this idea is that an investor in **ET** is automatically supporting a badly deprived sector of the future green solution, small unquoted companies with many of the best green ideas. Many of the larger companies themselves would be encouraged to set up unquoted offshoots with the financial backing of **ET**. And the investor is not giving any of his money away. He or she retains an investment with the prospect of delivering a good return. Should **ET** reach anything like its potential this would be a huge amount of money and give a tremendous boost to new environmental technologies. There are lots of good ideas out there that never see the light of day. Alternative energy sectors such as Solar Energy is one very obvious underfunded sector. A **Green Ventures Fund** linked to **ET** would ensure a consistent supply of funding to companies committed to developing such technologies into marketable solutions. *Let's give them a bit of sunshine.*

'Why ET Can Have A Mass Market Appeal'

As an index fund based on the main stock market index **ET** can be considered a mainstream investment offering a security comparable to any other 'blue chip' fund. It can appeal as a mass investment product rather than a niche product. It can replace existing investments which can be switched into **ET** without incurring any significant degree of extra risk. Indeed, **ET** will aim to clearly demonstrate why the fund will be pursuing the safest course of investment, as environmental pressures on business from Government and from consumers encroach more and more on their 'bottom line'.

Given the choice, it is difficult to see why investors who are concerned for the environmental impact of their investments would prefer a conventional environmental fund over **ET** or why those concerned with long term performance would prefer a conventional index fund over **ET**.

ET will be perfectly suitable for the full range of investment mediums: pensions, PEP'S, life assurance, unit and investment trusts funds. There is no logical reason why environmental investing cannot come to dominate every stock market in which this type of fund operates and change profoundly the priority given by business to its environmental responsibilities.

Enter 'The Mechanics Of Corporate Environmental Scoring'

The most challenging aspect of the **ET Mechanism** is the scoring system.

How can the **ESP** environmentally score a company using a transparent and widely canvassed criteria that can be reduced to 10 measurable criteria? Of course, this is not a question that can ever be definitively answered, and one of the functions of a broadly based panel is to refine the criteria and techniques for judging performance continuously.

However, there is now a wealth of expertise and committed organisations trying to encourage business to green itself. They are using many solid and objective indicators of how seriously a company is approaching its environmental responsibilities. Why not use that pool of expertise to create a viable, co-ordinated and comprehensive assessment? Those involved would only be too pleased to see their largely unpublicised efforts given a higher profile and the application of their ranking to a range of **ET** Funds would ensure that the decisive power of the financial system was supporting those efforts. This is the breakthrough that this proposal would offer. This would not be some toothless talking shop making advisory suggestions. Its ranking would become a real force in the business and financial world with real consequences

Enter 'The ESP Criteria'

An easily identifiable 10 point criteria is proposed. The logic of the criteria that is outlined here is not based on an ultimate ideal of what the ultimate green company would look like: otherwise they would all get zero and we wouldn't be able to rank them! That would be pointless. The point is to identify what the most committed companies are already doing, and highlight which companies are doing the least. This is not an 'ivory tower' scoring system. Each of the criteria have been included because to some degree, some companies are already doing those things. When **ET** has had the effect of encouraging the majority of companies to adopt those measures, the criteria can be refined ever upwards. This is the suggested initial criteria:

1. Has the company adopted an **Environmental Management System (EMS)**?

2. Does the company have an **Energy Efficiency Programme**?

3. Does it publish an annual **Environmental Report**?

4. Has it subjected new and existing products/services to comprehensive **Life Cycle Analysis** techniques and will it publish **Annual Environmental Accounts** on the basis of those company-wide Life Cycle Analyses?

5. Does it have a **Waste Reduction/Recycling Increase Programme**?

6. Does it have an **Environmental Purchasing Policy**?

7. Has it avoided any **Prosecutions or Regulatory Notices** for breaches of environmental responsibilities?

8. What percentage of its profits are vulnerable to current and anticipated **environmental liabilities**?

9. What evidence can the company show of **anticipating environmental pricing** pressures and proposing constructive alternatives to Government and Trade bodies?

10. What percentage of its profits are **donated to environmental and social causes**?

Each one of these criteria is further developed in the next scene. It would be open to the panel to consider whether each criteria should have equal weighting or whether one key criteria should be dominant. The author's own preference would be for the ninth criteria - initiatives by companies to lobby for environmental pricing - to account for more than 10% of the total score because this will be the key to which companies successfully adapt their business to the new environment.

It should be apparent that, with the exception of the last criteria, a company is not being asked to do anything that contradicts its search for profitability. Our aim is not to force a company to do things that could put it out of business. Instead the aim is to encourage them to do everything possible to protect the environment within the bounds of commercial logic. The solution for encouraging companies to adopt measures that are currently unprofitable is to lobby for the introduction of environmental pricing measures that will *make* them profitable. That way, the greenest companies automatically become the most profitable. This argument is absolutely pivotal which is why it is proposed as a key part of the criteria.

For anyone who objects to environmental performance being reduced to a score the question is: do they have a better answer? If so, let's hear it. For us, the advantages are obvious. It is systematic and it is transparent. Everybody, from the investor to the company can see what objectives are being set. The rankings and the sub scores that produced the rankings, will be published and if any company feels they have been unfairly scored they can respond with relevant evidence.

The whole of the next scene is devoted to detailing how the criteria would be applied in practice.

'Who sits at the table?'

The membership of the panel has been designed for maximum cross-fertilisation of opinion, spanning environmentalists, business experts and even political representatives. The role of the **ESP**, as well as carrying out the scoring exercise, would be to ensure that the criteria represents the sum of the best available thinking on the subject, and to serve as an open channel for all interested parties to put forward new ideas on how business can meet its environmental challenges. The panel would be systematically asking, what should a company be doing to improve its environmental impact?

Once established, the **ESP** would become an independent, autonomous structure within the mechanism. The key element of the panel's membership is its balance between representatives of leading environmental and business organisations. To ensure that balance is preserved, it is suggested that once established any change in categories of membership or scoring criteria would require a two thirds majority.

It is intended that the **ESP** membership be structured as follows:

Environmental Organisations - 9 places
Greenpeace 2
Friends of the Earth 2
Environmental Law Association 1
Environmental Investigation Agency 1
Academic Representatives 4 (to be chosen by each of the above in consultation with the Chairman of the Panel)

Business Organisations - 9 Places
Business in the Environment 1
100 Group of Finance Directors 1
Institute of Directors Environmental Sub Committee 1
Confederation of British Industry Environmental Sub committee 1
Association of Certified Cost Accountants (ACCA) 1
British Standards Institute Environmental Committee 1
Industry Specialists 4 (to be chosen by each of the above in consultation
with the Chairman of the Panel) with recognised expertise in the listed
scoring criteria, such as Life Cycle Analysis, Environmental Accounts,
Environmental Law etc....

Political Representatives- (as observers) 4
An Environmental Expert from each of the three main political parties
plus the Green Party.

Total Membership - 22

The panel will be jointly chaired by two members of the London School
of Economics Environmental Initiatives Network (LSEEIN) which was
founded in 1995 as part of the Schools Centenary Celebration. The network
has an eminent worldwide network of leading Environmental practitioners
from which to make a choice, which can be rotated annually, and has no
affiliation to any existing business or environmental organisation. **The
Environmental Investment Organisation** (EIO Ltd.), a non profit making
body that was formed in April 1996 by some of the founding members of
the network and is described in more detail below, will be responsible, in
consultation with the LSEEIN committee, for making the appointments.

The purpose of the panel would be initially to score and rank every company
in the FTSE index, although the methodology can be applied to all sizes
of company, in all markets, the FTSE being the prototype. The logic here
is that the largest companies have the greatest influence on the rest of the
economy and are therefore the place to start. Once this seed has been
sown, it can spawn clones all around the world.

The ranking of the largest companies on the stock market according to a
common environmental criteria is an activity of great benefit in its own
right, allowing a company's green commitment to be seen at a glance by
all interested groups.

Consumers, in particular, would be able to take a more informed decision on the companies they could be buying from, compared with the existing plethora of 'green marketing claims' which do not necessarily equate with a company's overall impact and commitment to the environment. It is, in fact, extending the principle of 'life cycle analysis', which is explained further in the following scene, to an entire company instead of isolated products which is how 'green consumerism' is often currently understood. The rankings can expect to achieve considerable publicity which would accentuate the benefit to a company of improving its score. Connecting the **ranking** of the **ESP** with a range of stock market index funds is simply a logical step which enables the *all-pervasive* effect of capital to be directed towards desirable green objectives.

Enter 'EIO - The Environmental Investment Organisation'

An **Environmental Scoring Panel,** as well as being a valid idea in its own right, would be necessary to establish the rankings on which **ET** would operate.

The risk in simply publishing this proposal before it is actually up and running in some form has always been that it would be used as little more than a marketing tool, without there being too much concern for the integrity of the end result. For the **ET Concept** to reach its full potential, a single authoritative ranking needs to be established and then made available to the financial institutions.

To avoid these risks it would be preferable for the launch of **ET** to be coordinated by a *new* investment organisation which does nothing else but promote green investing. It would be an exclusively *environmental* investment organisation, hence the **EIO - the Environmental Investment Organisation.**

The **EIO** was formed on St. Georges Day in 1996 as a non-profit making body with the task of coordinating the setting up of the **Environmental Scoring Panel** and coordinating the launch of the **ET Concept.** It need not be involved in the day to day operation of any funds. This could easily be 'contracted out' to existing fund management groups that specialise in index funds who can simply reweight the FTSE100 index, and every other index, according to the rankings of the **ESP.** Similarly the administration of investors purchases and sales can be easily 'contracted out' to existing fund management groups. These contracts would in time become very large and ought to attract the interest of those financial groups with the foresight to grasp the opportunity.

The **EIO** might therefore engage in joint ventures with existing fund management groups and arrangements such as subcontracting out day to day operational activities, but to preserve the integrity of the ideas and their ultimate intention the **EIO** would have to be an independent organisation. It would then be free to launch other green initiatives in the financial markets, in the UK and *globally*, and become a significant 'lobbying force' for environmental initiatives, backed by the weight of money.

The Marketing of ET

One can envisage the **ET Concept** being marketed to four separate audiences.

The General Public - a blue chip fund serving an environmental purpose can expect to have wide appeal. It could be structured for a whole range of personal investment products - pensions, PEPS, life assurance, unit and investment trusts.

Financial Institutions - a commitment to investing 1% or more of their assets under management in **ET** would be the initial target. This is a modest initial target, given the risk profile of the fund. Such a commitment would certainly help improve their public image of the investment world. Financial organisations in the charitable and public domain can be expected to agree to much larger commitments. An Investment Trust Structure would be the obvious initial launch structure.

Company Pension Schemes - such a fund would be ideal for companies wanting to invest their own money in a manner that supports their own environmental efforts and presents a very practical route for the 'stakeholder' philosophy to develop. Its risk profile again should present no conflict with their fiduciary responsibilities. Indeed, it is actually a requirement of a proper Environmental Management System to subject purchases, including the investment of the company's assets, to a green assessment!

Wealthy individuals - The problem with institutions is that even if everyone in an organisation agrees that something is a good idea they can be so bureaucratic that it can take months, even *years*, for them to act. Wealthy individuals have no such constraints. Given that many of them already have large amounts already invested in the stock market, and have publicly-stated green sympathies, it might not be too difficult to persuade them to invest in something very similar to what they are already investing in, with the noble *added benefit* of serving a positive environmental purpose. There are lots of extremely wealthy individuals who would be very interested in putting some of their money behind their sympathies. At the moment most of that money is either swishing around the financial markets doing anything but that or having a marginal effect in existing green and ethical funds.

Such people might be the key to getting the whole thing off the ground. In recognition of this a separate and informal network has been set up under the name of the **'WorldWide Millionaires Environmental Network'** with the task of obtaining backing and support for the **EIO** and other green initiatives.

'Enter EIO On The Global Investment Stage'

The purpose of the **EIO** is to extend the **ET** method internationally as soon as possible. Although a UK debut is looking most likely there is no reason why it could not be launched in any other Stock market. America, Europe and Japan would be the next major targets. The principle could be extended to a range of Global **ET's,** for example based on the FT Global 500, to be known as **GET**. One could devise an **ET** for all those fashionable emerging markets where one gets the impression the fund management companies do not know there is an environment, never mind a potentially life threatening crisis on the planet.

Would it not be most fitting if London would have led the world again with this particular financial innovation. Let's face it, London has been responsible for billions of pounds worth of bad environmental consequences across the planET over the last century and a half. It would be nice to think it could begin to even up the balance sheet. Touché!

'A Summary Of The Scene So Far'

1) The **Environmental Tracking Concept** is a simple combination of the merits of indexation with an overlay of environmental scoring.

2) It could only work once an independent **Environmental Scoring Panel** made up of experts across the environmental and business spectrum and specifically including green pressure groups had been set up and published a transparent Environmental Ranking.

3) **ET** would require a new investment organisation to be set up called the **EIO**, the **Environmental Investment Organisation.** It would be a purely environmental investment organisation and can develop spin offs from its core activity, in particular a **GREEN VENTURES FUND.**

4) Once launched **ET** could achieve mass appeal and grow to a very significant size. It is anticipated it would be launched in the UK stock market first but the concept could be quickly extended throughout the planET.

5) As environmental issues continue to climb the human agenda a target of 51% of the assets in each stock market being managed under the **ET** criteria is not inconceivable.

6) The **ET** concept can play a significant and radical role in spreading sustainable environmental practices throughout the planetary EcoMony.

'When Does The Performance Begin?'

Readers may be interested to know that since this book was originally written significant progress has already been made in setting up the first ranking of the FTSE 100. The original text of this book was presented to several senior directors of **Greenpeace International** in December 94. Although unable to give a definite response at the time of writing to the invitation to join the **Environmental Scoring Panel,** Greenpeace nevertheless forwarded the idea to John Elkington of Sustainability Ltd., who in collaboration with **Business In the Environment**, have produced the first pilot ranking of the FTSE 100. The **EIO** is at the time of publication appointing the first joint chairpersons the **Environmental Scoring Panel** from the membership of the **London School of Economics Environmental Iniatives Network** for the U.K. Appointments for the **ESP** in America, Australia, Canada and several European countries are being planned through the extensive international membership of the LSE network. Meanwhile the BIE questionaire is expected to form the basis of the **ESP ranking** for the purposes of launching a range of **ET index funds** in the U.K.

Is all this really feasible?

Are we talking *planetary transformation? Or just Acorns.*

Maybe both! Either there is some gigantic flaw in this plot - which try as we might we cannot see - or **ET**, and other funds set up to use the **ESP** rankings, could rapidly grow to the target point of owning 51% of the shares on the worlds major stock markets.

Then the language of money would really be 'talking green' all round the planet.

And since at the present moment, money exercises great power that makes **ET** in principle a pretty damn good idea.

So. What are we waiting for? Xmas? Well, Merry Xmas and let's get on with it.

Scenery Change and Intermission.

ACT TWO
Scene 2

Re-Enter 'ESP -
The Environmental Scoring Panel'

The foregoing description of how **ET** could make its London debut, then go on to perform on the world stage, would appear to have demonstrated something slightly significant: a method for enabling the majority of the world's investors to invest in an index linked fund that promotes environmental objectives.

The purpose of this Scene is to provide an initial blueprint for the scoring mechanism on which all the advantages of the scheme ultimately depend. There is no point in creating a pressure in the stock market to change business behaviour if it does not actually deliver the desired goal: a healthier environment for the planet and everyone living in it. However, we should not expect perfect answers. We are talking about answers less imperfect than the present. And about carrots that will help us perfect the answers.

The concept of the fund itself, its mass appeal and its successful operation in the stock market is jumping out of the script into real life already. It's a marketing person's dream. The only question is: would a company that receives a higher score on the scoring criteria be better for the environment than one with a low score?

To ensure this, we would need all those environmental and business specialists, who are already playing their parts in all the existing iniatives, to take their parts in this mega-drama. We therefore need to demonstrate to them, point by point, how the **ESP** mechanism would work.

We do not wish to run the risk at this stage of boring anyone who has become enthused by the prospect of **ET** with a mass of detail on how the scoring would work. If you are already persuaded of the idea from the previous scene, our suggestion is: don't fall asleep during this one, just skip through it and move to the next ACT where we really start to have some fun with the stock market.

May we begin with some introductory comments.

'Measure For Measure'

The theme running throughout all the criteria is measurement. It means putting numbers to a conclusion. It may appear cold, rational and boring. Why do we need to measure? Because otherwise we are *guessing*. This was the crux of our criticism of the majority of existing green investment. And to be frank, of green thinking in general. *There is too much guesswork involved.* With something as important as the environment we have to be reasonably certain that any particular change that is being advocated can have a positive overall outcome. We cannot ultimately be certain of anything but our first priority, over and above any particular solution, is to encourage the search for the best solution. Which means being able to measure the facts before we make a change and the facts after the change. Which in the case of the environment is incredibly complex. But not impossibly complex, we hope, for open minded, intelligent men and women.

It might be nice to live in a world where such complexity did not exist; where billions of pounds, dollars and yen were not charging around the planet: then such an incredibly complex problem as the one this acorn is trying to solve would not exist. That would take us back many thousands of years. Since we do live in this age and are unlikely to return to that simple paradise, if it was, we have only one rational option: to measure the effect of everything we consume and the processes that produce them and replace them with things and methods that have a more positive effect on the environment. This concept is known as Life Cycle Analysis - **LCA**.

Introducing 'Life Cycle Analysis'

What is **LCA**? It is a method of establishing the most environmentally friendly way of producing a particular product or service by conducting a truly comprehensive 'cradle to grave' analysis of all the environmental impacts caused by a product, starting from obtaining the raw materials to producing them, to how the product is finally disposed of.

Although to date it has been mainly used for comparing the environmental merits of particular products, its ability to quantify the effects of different options can be the basis of a much wider use of the **LCA** method.

LCA and its counterpart, Environmental Impact Assessment, sits at the top of environmental solutions alongside Environmental Pricing. In fact, Environmental Pricing is not possible without **LCA**. In order to *compare* the environmental costs of a product we need a reliable method of measuring those costs. **LCA**, by *whatever name,* is the only thing that can do that and its development is essential if we wish to solve the environmental crisis. If that is true you may be wondering why the development of a reliable **LCA** model has not been a top Government priority throughout the world? Yet another sad case of our old friend, 'wood for the trees syndrome.'

The scoring mechanism of the **ESP** can be viewed as an **LCA** applied to an entire company, rather than its individual products.

For a consumer it is, of course, highly relevant to know which specific products have the lowest negative environmental impact. For an investor, the total picture is more important if we want to direct investment into those companies with the greatest demonstrable overall environmental commitment. Even for a conscientious consumer, this is highly relevant. They might be concerned to see that their money is buying the maximum environmental benefit and not supporting an organisation, which may look impressive on one or two particular products, without making any fundamental effort to develop its environmental commitment.

The question is: how can a total assessment be fairly and reliably arrived at?

Enter 'External Verifiers'

Wherever possible, the **ESP** would base its scoring methodology on existing initiatives using existing centres of expertise. Most of the criteria have been selected because a body already exists that is assessing the performance of companies against that particular criteria or there is an existing pool of expertise that can be called upon to assist in that process. The task of the **ESP** would be to co-ordinate those separate assessments into one ranking exercise, and fill the gaps.

In the case of an Environmental Management System - **EMS** - for example, the British Standards Institute has established a system of verification by accredited auditors. Likewise for the European Community's **EMS** scheme. In the case of Environmental reports, the Association of Certified Cost Accountants - ACCA - already holds an annual competition for all company environmental reports. Although no such competition exists for **LCA**, there are a number of organisations who are established in that field who would be well qualified to advise on such a review. Where an independent review does not yet exist, the **ESP** can liaise closely with existing centres of expertise in the particular criteria before coming to its final scoring methodology.

The great attraction of the Environmental Rankings the **ESP** would produce is that, for the first time, a company's environmental performance can be assessed in totality instead of as separate components. We can begin to see the wood as well as the trees!

'Is The Environment Becoming Another Excuse For More Bureaucracy?'

Unfortunately the truthful answer is yes, and the scoring exercise and many of the criteria could be accused of falling into that category. That fills us with no pleasure whatsoever. However, it brings us back to this getting from A to B problem. Given that we live in an absurdly complex world which has generated some absurdly complex problems, we have to start unravelling those complex problems now, in the world as we find it.

Let us start unravelling.

The ultimate solution for reducing bureaucracy is for individuals to be operating in an environment where their initiative and common sense is free to flourish. In such an environment, perhaps a complex criteria such as outlined below would not be necessary. But unfortunately we do not. We hope that getting people to think about the environment, at all levels, might take us a little closer to that ideal. It can actually become an opportunity for organisations to rethink their structures, and how they involve their staff in solving problems. Hopefully the criteria can develop so that companies, who demonstrate a less bureaucratic way of achieving environmental excellence are encouraged.

The purpose of the initial criteria is to get the ball rolling. As we get that ball rolling, we can think of ways of encouraging companies to involve their staff in their improvement programmes. The **ESP** does not have to rely exclusively on the 'official' version of events regarding the subject at hand. The results of the **ESP** are going to be published for each company. Any employee or interested party who feels the evidence that the **ESP** has received is not a true and fair picture of the reality on the ground ought to be encouraged to explain their view. The more a company involves people on the ground, the more effective the policy can become.

The process of scoring companies against an environmental criteria needs to be seen as an interim bureaucratic stage. The adoption of environmental pricing can save us all a great deal of this bureaucracy because it can start *incentivising* the desired result, without the need for a layer of bureaucratic environmental procedures on top of normal commercial pressures. Under an environmental pricing system, commercial pressures and environmental pressures will become one and the same. It appears we have to go through this intermediate stage to *prove* that a more fundamental solution would be *easier* for everyone.

Whatever 'solution' is being proposed, whether it be 'clean production strategies', 'reuse, repair, recycle', they can only succeed if *prices* incentivise companies to adopt them, and if their case can be proven by the use of comprehensive and comparative **LCA's** against the alternative methods.

If we cannot develop such a methodology based on the broadest possible consensus, we are simply replacing one dogma with another.

Re-Enter the Carrots- 'The ESP Criteria'

To recap from the last scene, the 10-point criteria proposed here is not based on an ultimate ideal of what the ultimate green company would look like: otherwise they would all get zero and we wouldn't be able to rank them. The point is to identify what the most committed companies are already doing, and highlight which companies are doing the least. This is not meant to be an 'ivory tower' scoring system. When **ET** has had the effect of encouraging the majority of companies to adopt those measures, the criteria can be refined ever upwards.

The first criteria asks if the company has implemented an Environmental Management System (EMS) which is becoming a central issue for green business. As with all the criteria, we are not expressing an opinion about how effective an EMS might actually be in practice. We are saying that it represents evidence of a commitment to improve, and should be recognised as a starting point, because *we have to start somewhere*. Since adopting an EMS is such a wide ranging policy, it is suggested that the 10 point criteria should include separate evidence of its key components being supported, as well as important criteria that are not included in an EMS.

This is important, because the one thing the **ESP** does not want to be guilty of is accepting 'bits of paper' as evidence of environmental commitment. The criteria is designed to look at *real* evidence and *real* measures. It was also necessary to adopt this 'look through' policy because many companies who have not formally adopted an EMS may still be implementing important components of it and ought to therefore be rewarded for that.

The criteria to date is as follows:

1. 'Does the company have an Environmental Management System - EMS?'

An **EMS** is a useful starting point for any organisation that wants to reduce its environmental impact. It institutionalises the actions necessary for that improvement. Those actions are no longer optional or discretionary. They are built into the organisation's systems. It does not have to be a 'top down' approach. It can become an opportunity for a company to start involving its workforce in how the company organises its activities. It is much more than a statement. No company can go to the trouble and expense of having a **EMS** and not be serious about it. It is not a one-off change. It is meant to be a process of continual improvement.

For example, in the UK, an **EMS** has been designed by the British Standards Institute. It is known as BS7750 Environmental Management

System. It was published in February 1994 after a two year trial period with a wide range of large and small companies. BS7750 is a ten page document which lists a range of activities necessary for a company to be accredited with this standard.

The first page of the document gives a definition of the terms used. The first term defined is 'continual improvement of environmental performance'. The document states that this is meant to include all measures that are 'economically viable'.

We need to understand from what was said in the earlier paragraph that a company cannot regularly afford to do something as a result of having an **EMS** that is more expensive than a less environmentally-friendly option. There are some companies who are so committed that they will go one step further and chose a more expensive option thereby sacrificing a bit of profit. But it still has to operate to a commercial discipline. Any company that pursued such a course of action to any serious degree would eventually go out of business. The point of the **ESP criteria** is not to put a company out of business but lobby for a structure in which companies can adapt.

Which bring us back to the concept of Environmental Pricing. We have to adjust the commercial discipline a company is responding to.

There is, however, a great deal that can and is being done under the current non environmental pricing system to improve the impact of business on the environment. The widespread use of an EMS would ensure that everything that can be done under the present rules under which companies operate is being done. *Which itself would be a huge step forward.* This is what is beginning to happen and what the **ESP** and the **ET** are designed to encourage.

The second definition is of the word 'environment'. It states that, "as the environmental effects of an organisation may reach all parts of the world the environment in this context extends from the workplace to the global eco system". The implications of this definition for business thinking and actions is utterly profound. Revolutionary if applied to its full potential. It implies some very big changes in the way business defines its obligations. Let's give business the opportunity to really act upon that statement.

The BS7750 is being used as a model of **EMS** for countries around the world.

To give some idea of what is involved in the proper implementation of an **EMS** the following is a summary of its main requirements:

* a publicly available environmental policy to be formulated;
* the appointment of key personnel to implement the policy;
* the dissemination of the policy throughout all levels of the organisation and to subcontractors;
* a register of all environmental effects caused by the organisation;
* procedures for responding to external enquires on those effects;
* a record of all applicable regulatory requirements;
* the setting of objectives beyond the minimum regulatory requirements within the company's commercial ability;
* a management programme to implement the foregoing;
* a manual to document how the foregoing shall be implemented;
* and maintain proper records of all of the forgoing for external verification;
* and establish a management *audit* programme to establish compliance with all of the foregoing;
* and conduct management *reviews* of the Environmental Management Systemestablished to comply with BS7750 and assess whether it allows the company to meet its commitment to "continuous improvement".

This is a formidable range of requirements,(although lacking any serious carrots) designed to ensure that a company accredited with this standard is making significant inroads into its environmental impacts. It remains to be seen whether this is the result in practice and whether its methods are practical, but its intentions need surely be recognised as serious.

The BS7750 document goes into greater detail on these points in an annexe. Of particular note is its emphasis on ensuring some effort is made to assess the environmental suitability of suppliers. It also states that a company should consider if its financial assets are invested in a manner consistent with its environmental policy. **ET should be perfect.**

Unfortunately, the annexe specifically states that the adoption of Life Cycle Analysis techniques is not necessary for a company to achieve the standard.

Nor is their any requirement to publish an annual environmental report or the results of internal or external audits of the company's environmental performance.

(BS7750 is not the only **EMS** scheme companies may adopt. The European Community's **EMS** directive has different criteria. The ISO, the international equivalent of the BSI, is also adopting an **EMS** which companies can be accredited with.)

The panel will have to confirm whether a full score can automatically be awarded to any company that has an externally accredited EMS. Companies who have implemented an EMS that has not been externally accredited, or have implemented key components of it, in particular a programme of environmental audits, could receive up to half the maximum score, according to the best assessment the members of the **ESP** are able to make of that company's efforts from the evidence provided.

Let us continue down the list of the **ESP** criteria.

2. 'Does the company have an energy efficiency policy?'

This needs no explanation other than to say that huge savings are consistently achieved by companies who have set energy reduction targets. Furthermore, this will place those companies in the least vulnerable position to the inevitable rise in energy prices that will follow from higher energy taxes. It will also encourage companies to explore alternative, non polluting forms of energy.

3. 'Does the company publish an annual Environmental Report?'

Also, not something required in the BS7750 **EMS** but an important additional piece of evidence through which a company can publicly demonstrate its actions. If it is making a serious effort to improve its environmental performance, it surely has nothing to fear from publishing an environmental report.

As already suggested, their is already an annual review of environmental reports which could provide the basis for the score given under this criteria.

Half the points for this criteria could be awarded automatically to any company publishing an Environmental Report. The other half could be apportioned according to the quality of the report, as assessed by the current competition.

4. 'Does the company use LCA techniques and does the company publish Annual Environmental Accounts?'

The pivotal importance of **LCA** has already been explained and some suggestions made about how it could develop in the future. Environmental Accounts is not the same thing as an Environmental Report.

The objective here is to encourage companies to quantify their total environmental impact. This is the extension of the methodology of **LCA** to the company's activities in their entirety. It is, in fact, the simple aggregate of all the **LCA** impacts identified across the company's product/ service range. This criteria will not therefore be achievable until a company is able to maintain up-to-date **LCA's** on its entire output. However, if we want to move forward from guesswork to accuracy, it is the only way forward.

This criteria has the double advantage of both encouraging companies to adopt a full **LCA** of all activities and giving the **ESP** a very clear and comparative view of a company's total environmental impact.

Any company that can produce a set of annual environmental accounts ought to receive an automatic maximum score. A discretionary score of up to half the maximum could be awarded by the panel to any company whose effort in the **LCA** field is judged to have made a significant step towards the publication of Annual Environmental Accounts.

Would it follow that companies with the highest impact scores will be the least successful? Not necessarily. It depends how they adapt. It depends what counter proposals they make to Government to ensure that the same end functions and services are achieved but in a manner that reduces those environmental impacts and from which they can profit. It's all about solutions. Does it matter how much profit someone makes from solving environmental problems if the economy is structured to benefit the environment? The study of economics has taught us that companies, and people, tend to solve problems when they can make a profit from doing so.

There are several centres of expertise on **LCA** from which to find a representative for the panel and several individual experts prominent in the field.

5. 'What percentage of its profits are vulnerable to current and anticipated environmental liabilities?'

This is one of the key impacts on a company's bottom line but also very hard to predict. The extent to which a company becomes liable for historical or current pollution damage is a question of legal and ultimately political judgement. It seems unlikely that companies will be forced to take on legal liabilities from activities that at the time were not illegal. Rather, penalties and taxes will be used to ensure that those activities are deterred. However, there will be grey areas and an element of risk. It is therefore a precautionary criteria to ensure that the worst possible liability scenario is reflected in the panel's scoring.

There already exist commercial attempts to gauge a companies exposure to environmental liabilities and it assumed that the panel will make use of those assessments in arriving at its score.

6. 'Does it have a waste reduction/recycling increase programme?'

These are already widespread and many positive developments have come from these programmes. Companies adopting such a programme invariably find themselves saving money in ways they had not previously identified. They often find themselves discovering some new process or cost saving that they are then able to market to other companies. Environmental literature is littered with hundreds of examples. To quote but one, Toshiba, the Japanese company, discovered a method of converting all types of plastic back into its original form - petroleum. It stands to make millions of yen, not only from its own cost savings, but from marketing this breakthrough throughout the world.

A company that can demonstrate the application of a Waste Reduction/ Recycling Increase programme could automatically receive half the maximum score. The other half could be apportioned according to the quality of the programme as assessed from the evidence.

7. 'Does it have an environmental purchasing policy?'

Encouraging the largest companies in each economy to adopt such a policy could have a profoundly beneficial effect throughout the ecomony. They are everybody else's most important customers. The effect of this spur cannot be overstated.

The Chartered Institute of Purchasing and Supply, who collaborated in the writing of the Business in the Environment publication, *"Buying Into The Environment"*, would be a natural source of expertise in this field.

Half the maximum score could be awarded to any company that could demonstrate evidence of implementing such a policy. The other half could be apportioned according to the quality of the evidence as assessed by the Panel.

8. 'Has it avoided any prosecutions or regulatory notices for breaches of environmental responsibilities.'

Companies breaching environmental legislation are already finding the fines and the public spotlight increasing. We can safely say that the scale of fines is heading in one clear direction-north- and the impact on the bottom line in the opposite direction-south. Its inclusion in the **ESP** ranking exercise should turn up that spotlight and **ET** can back it with financial pressure in the stock market.

The Environmental Law Association is a natural source of expertise in this field and it is hoped a representative from the Association as well as one of the many leading Law firms specialising in the field of environmental law can be invited to sit on the panel.

Any company avoiding any regulatory breach in its previous twelve months could automatically receive a maximum score. The panel could still award a discretionary score of up to half the maximum in rare cases where the breach is a one off and considered minor, as indicated by the relevant Regulatory body.

9. 'Can it show evidence of constructive proposals to Government/ Trade bodies for raising environmental standards through environmental pricing, LCA research or other measures?'

This criteria is designed to encourage companies to actually become part of the movement campaigning for higher environmental standards. This is a unique and vital innovative element in the criteria. Too often forward thinking companies find their efforts to introduce some new technology or method thwarted by current rules or pricing arrangements. It is vital that every time such an obstacle is reached they do not just put the idea on the shelf and wait for somebody else to lobby government.

Similarly, instead of being at the receiving end of legislation or fiscal incentives/disincentives that might not be the best solution, they could be using their first hand experience of the situation to say what is the best solution. It is a logical extension of the concept of 'corporate responsibility' that companies become active participants in the search for solutions. By abdicating this role they are withholding a valuable source of expertise from the debate on how the EcoNomy is to move to an EcoMony, as well as damaging their own interests and those of their shareholders.

There needs to be a willingness to explore bold solutions that they could then become part of. If they want to be in a business that will continue to grow the answer is simple; develop strategies that serve an environmental purpose and suggest ways to incentivise that strategy. Who can criticise a company for presenting well researched alternatives to the status quo if a genuine environmental improvement can be demonstrated?

Some of these solutions would involve a shift to 'clean technology' and a fundamental rethink about how the company produces its products. If a company can show that marginal changes in the current fiscal/regulatory regime would enable it to do so, it should find many sources of support by stating this in public. (We need a very serious discussion about EcoLogical Carrots!)

The obvious sources of expertise in this field, and many others, are the leading Environmental Campaign groups, Greenpeace and Friends of the Earth foremost amongst them. Greenpeace recently released a new study on 'Clean Production' and how it could apply to Poland, as a model for the rest of Eastern Europe. How about as a model for Western Europe as well? Let's start implementing a *total solution*.

A representative from each of these organisations will be invited to sit on the panel and it would be an absolute tragedy if they were to turn down such an opportunity. Greenpeace and Friends of the Earth have developed an impressive expertise in engaging business in the discussion of how to adapt to the green challenge on the ground and their input would be key to the success of the **ESP**.

It is suggested that the panel also extend an open invitation to the three main political parties, and of course the Green Party, to have a Member of Parliament or other official representative with expertise in the environmental field to sit on the panel, perhaps in an observer role.

Evidence of 'constructive proposals' and 'proactive campaigning' would be a difficult area to score and would lend itself to the 'qualative assessment approach' rather than yes/no scoring, but perhaps any company that can demonstrate a constructive proposal or response, in accordance with the above as assessed by the panel, could be given an automatic score of one half of the maximum. The other half should be apportioned according to the quality and volume of the proposals as assessed by the **ESP**.

10. 'What percentage of its profits are donated to environmental causes?'

This would be the icing on the cake for green investors. Not only would they be encouraging a comprehensive environmental improvement amongst companies, but they would be giving companies an incentive to donate a percentage of their profits to conservation and environmental projects at home, and around the world.

To minimise difficulties defining which charities and causes can be classified as environmental, the term could be interpreted in the widest possible sense of the word. Thus donations to the Arts or Health charities could all be considered contributions under this criteria since they are, at least in my book, part of an effort to raise quality of life, which I consider indistinguishable from quality of environment. In effect, there would be very few charitable donations that would not be included. Given that any contribution is a worthy act for a company, this need not in any way detract from the positive effect of rewarding companies for such behaviour.

An existing conservation group would be a natural source of expertise the panel could draw on, such as the World Wildlife Fund. Companies donating a fraction of the sale price of a good or service to conservation projects around the world could also be included when assessing donations as a percentage of profits. Perhaps this criteria could even be used to encourage trade carried out on the growing network of **LET's** systems and would provide a valuable link between traditional business and the greener elements of the economy.

In this case the score given would need to be based on a straight ranking of the percentage of profits donated to environmental causes as defined above. The rankings would be divided into 10 sub groups and scores of between 1 and 10 given to each company according to which sub group their position in the ranking placed them in. It is open to possibility that an element of the score would be from a qualitative assessment of where the company had donated its grant and the reasons it put forward for doing so.

That concludes the discussion of the scoring criteria of the **ESP**.

All in all, a pretty serious carrot for everyone to chew on before jumping to any knee jerk conclusions about.

Is it too bureaucratic? Well, if the prize is directing a few trillion dollars in a more environmentally acceptable direction, we assert it is a practical starting point!

'Into the Future'

The **ESP**, as conceived here, is intended to serve as the model for every stock mark**ET** in the world. It is the prototype. If it can operate as described here in the UK, it can, with a certain amount of adjustment for local conditions, be replicated in other countries.

Indeed, the FTSE100 Index, which accounts for about 8% of the world stock market capitalisation, is the most international index in the world because of the extent to which the largest UK companies have expanded abroad. The initial work of the **ESP** would already involve applying its criteria to every corner of the globe.

For the UK, and in due course other markets, the option would be open to extend the ranking exercise to lower tiers of the market; firstly the mid

250 index of companies in the UK and then eventually the remainder of the FT allshare index. This would be a necessary prelude to the launch of an **ET** for lower tiers of the stock market. The practicality of whether such a detailed scoring criteria could be simplified for smaller sized companies is an issue to be addressed in the future. Let's get to B first.

The point that is worth re-emphasising is that smaller companies respond to the wishes of their bigger customers. *The largest companies in any economy are clearly the place to start for the maximum effect in the shortest time.* This is why a multinational **ESP** would be the next priority. To be followed by an **ESP** for the USA, Japan, Europe and Developing Asia.

We can see no reason why an **ESP** Panel could not be set up for the largest 100 Public Sector organisations. They are almost completely unaccountable for their environmental behaviour. **Which is scandalous!**

'Re-Enter Money As We Leave This ACT'

The argument, rightly or wrongly, comes back down to money.

If a company's ability to raise capital is being affected by investment patterns based on its ranking by the **ESP**, it would have to take the **ESP** seriously. Whether a company's ability to raise capital is affected by its environmental ranking depends on how big **ET** becomes and how quickly.

If a company's sales are suffering because of its ranking by the **ESP**, it would be forced to improve that ranking. That depends on how effectively the **ESP** publicises its rankings. We do not anticipate that being a problem. It's such a simple thing to publicise. Rank the top 100 companies according to their total environmental record, list all their products, and let green consumer pressure do the rest. The companies themselves may want to use their position in the rankings to promote themselves against competitors. And why not? Don't we want the criteria to be more widely adopted?

Anyone reading between the lines can see that the criteria is no soft option. It's full adoption by the largest companies in each economy could transform the role of business in solving the environmental crisis, and create yet more radical possibilities.

The message is wonderfully clear to every company in the FTSE100, and in due course to companies in every other stock market in the world. Get a top ranking and you have a marketing person's dream to exploit. Get a bottom ranking on the **ESP** assessment and it could be a commercial disaster. Which is precisely the intention. It's 'survival of the environmentally fittest' and someone has to come last. If a company does come last, could its business ever shake off such an image? Well. There is one sure way of putting the image right again. Come top of the **ESP** rankings next time round.

That's a comp**ET**itive environmental pressure.

Some people have said why can't the rankings be divided into groups of 10, given that no scoring system could ever be perfect. That way no company would actually come top, or bottom. We have the ten worst and best environmental companies but we *don't* have a top and bottom spot. Safety in numbers! That reminds us of those debates amongst educationalists. Nobody should come last! We think in this case a **'star pupil'** and a **'dunce cap'** is precisely what we need. We keep being told how necessary competition is; how the best must be rewarded and the weak have to go to the wall. Well, let's apply a bit of that philosophy to the protection of the environment. Can anything but good come of it? A bottom and a top spot. Every year. With **ET** behind it, we'll soon see some serious action.

Does it make sense or does it make sense? It makes **ESP**.

ACT TWO
Scene 3

What Are The Implications Of A Global ET?

In asking this question I am keenly aware that it has little meaning unless this concept can make the leap from proposal to reality. What are the chances of that happening?

The potential of the concept is very clear in terms of both speed and scale of implementation, simply because of the ease with which the financial industry could participate for its own self interest. However advocating a feasible idea, of universal benefit to all its participants in concrete financial terms, as well as the infinitely more important ecological ones, is no guarantee of success.

We have a mechanism here that has been designed to apply to the FTSE100 Index of the London Stock Market. Since all stock markets and their respective indexes operate to the same principle, it follows that with very little adaption the concept could be applied to any stock market.

This would require the setting up of local Environmental Scoring Panels based on the participation of the leading Environmental and Business Groups. Which is what makes the involvement of Greenpeace and Friends of the Earth so critical since they are uniquely endowed with an international network covering virtually every part of the planet.

As well as giving rise to a series of national **ETs**, a network of **ESP's** across the planet would enable an international index to be designed and a corresponding **Global ET** Fund. Were such a fund, comprising of perhaps the five hundred largest companies in the world, to become a dominant force in world stock markets, we would indeed be talking about an 'Investment Revolution' able to make a decisive contribution to the solution of the ecological crisis before us. We would have a form of 'stakeholder democracy', backed, not by voluntary, dare I say tokensitic declarations, by corporate PR departments, but by a direct accountability between the managers of these corporations and their investing public. Environmental achievements would become their motivating culture and a failure to steer their organisation to meet that challenge would be met by an ultimate sanction, replacement.

What the implications of these global developments might be, seems so far removed at present that the question arises as to whether contemplating its future development on such a scale is a wise use of energy, when it might be more usefully applied ensuring that the very first stage itself is actually accomplished.

How could the **EIO,** a very small organisation with miniscule resources, attempting to take the first steps towards the formation of an **ESP** for the UK, engineer such a breathtaking assault on the citadels of financial power? Well, as that ancient chinese proverb reminds us, a journey of a thousand miles has to begin with a single footstep. The first public step in the **EIO's** journey was a press announcement, made on the 23rd April 1997, the date of its first anniversary and the also the anniversary of St George, Patron Saint of England, and legendary slayer of dragons.

The statement read:

"EIO LAUNCHES NEW GREEN INVESTMENT CONCEPT FOR ORDINARY INVESTORS"

The ENVIRONMENTAL INVESTMENT ORGANISATION- was formed one year ago as a non profit body dedicated to operating within the financial system to bring the environmental challenge into the heart of business and financial thinking. It is choosing today, the 23rd April 1997, the first anniversary of its formation, to announce a new investment concept known as 'Environmental Tracking'. The new investment concept is a hybrid between a conventional green fund and an index tracking fund and has been designed to operate in any major stock market. The concept is being initially announced in London in recognition of its pre-eminent position in global fund management. The thinking behind the new concept is fully explained in a new book to be published shortly under the title:

'ENVIRONMENTAL TRACKING' CAN INVESTMENT REVOLUTION PREVENT ECOLOGICAL CATASTROPHE

*The **EIO** is launching the **ET** concept with a campaign to persuade city institutions to commit 1% or more of funds under management into the **ET** concept TO MARK ITS CONTRIBUTION TO THE CELEBRATION OF THE year 2000. In support of the campaign, the **EIO** has identified six endorsement groups who will be asked to promote a public campaign in support of the commitment to ET of 1% under the headline;*

'ET WANTS 1% TOWARDS THE PLANET'S RENT'

The purpose of the endorsement groups is to promote the concept proposed in the book with an unusually high and diverse level of endorsement which it would be very difficult for existing financial organisations to ignore. The proposal has been designed to sell itself as an exciting marketing opportunity for those financial organisations with the foresight to support this effort to give real teeth to the lip service so often found in corporate environmental thinking.

*The six endorsement groups from which the **EIO** is actively recruiting support have been categorised for convenience as:*

City Figures and Financial Commentators
Environmental organisations and experts
Green thinking business organisations and practitioners
Academics of all disciplines with Environmental sympathies
Media, Artistic and Sports Celebrities
Political Figures of all parties

Up to twenty people from each category will be asked to endorse the project in a Media Statement to publicise that endorsement.

*The **EIO** has close links with another recently formed organisation known as the **London School of Economics Environmental Initiatives Network (LSEEIN)** which was formed at the time of the schools centenary celebration in 1995 to promote initiatives in the environmental field. One* *of the key components of the ET Concept is the formation of a broadly based independent 'Environmental Scoring Panel' comprised of experts from across the environmental and business spectrum. The EIO intends to approach the LSEEIN with a view to seeking two suitable individuals from its extensive and eminent membership to jointly chair the workings of the Environmental Scoring Panel.*

And so the journey began. And slowly but surely, the fish began to bite. And why wouldn't they? **ET** has been designed to make sense to all the major participants in the environmental/financial problem. So unless the world has gone completely insane, there really is no logical reason why **ET** cannot fullfil its objectives.

The key to engineering that transition from concept to reality is the achievement of the first stated goal of the **EIO**, the committment by the financial community of 1% of funds under management by the year 2000 to the **ET Concept**. If the approach of the year 2000 is not sufficient spur to galvanise its particpants into waking up to their responsibilities, it is difficult to see what could.

And if they cannot agree to the fractional sum of 1% of funds under management, then frankly, we really are in trouble, and we really do have the wrong people in the wrong positions. 1% is a litmus test. And it needs to be 1%, or nothing. 1% is the only realistic base from which Environmental Tracking can build for the future.

Of course, although London has been given a head start, it is open to any financial centre to take the lead and make that committment by the year 2000. This wouldn't be the first idea to have been developed in these islands and launched elsewhere.

Wherever it is launched, I am perfectly clear as the author of this concept that 1% is the non negotiable minimum commitment that is needed from any financial community to give this project a chance of success. Anything less would be a token deception.

What are the chances of that initial stated objective being achieved? What are the chances that before the year 2000, the **EIO** will be in a position to publicise which organisations have been persuaded to put their signature to that commitment and those who have not.

What are the chances of the environmental movement finding the vision to unite behind the aims of an investment concept? What are the chances of the world's leading investment organisations embracing this opportunity to become the champions rather than the villains of the future? What are the chances of the great mass of ordinary people, as investors, as consumers, as voters, as citizens of the future, grasping what is at stake and taking the trouble to understand how this ultimately very simple proposal can work?

Well if I knew the answer to those questions, I guess I really would be on a different planet.

And now, for those flexible enough to cope, may I take a detour from the somewhat demanding nature of these questions and present:
                                        'something completely different...'

ACT THREE
And Now For Something Completely Different

Scene 1
'The Humour Tracking Concept'

In this final Act we step back from the serious purpose behind 'Environmental Tracking' and consider the merits of Humour Tracking.

It may or not surprise the reader to know that this last Act has caused more controversy than just about any other part of the book. Its inclusion is not meant to detract from the seriousness of what has been said before but rather to offer a lighter angle for those punters who prefer life not to be *too* serious *all* the time.

Enter The Three J's

Who are the three 'J's'? They are **'Jip'** and **'Jif'** and **'Jim'**.

'Jip' is the **JOKE INVESTMENT PANEL.** **'Jif'** is the **JOKE INDEX FUND.** **'Jim'** is short for, of course, **JOKE INVESTMENT MANAGEMENT**.

Having shown in Act 1 an index that can be re-weighted by applying a clear and transparent criteria to the companies in the index, it seems reasonable to consider what other noble causes could be promoted by such a hybrid?

What is being proposed here is a mirror image of '**ET**' and '**ESP**', which we hope everyone accepts are perfectly sensible ideas, with an index fund that tracks the FTSE 100 index for humour, which might appear to some people to be a silly idea. But is it?

Jip would reweight companies according to how extensively they incorporate humour into their corporate culture.

The investment logic here is that humour, as well as being a very good thing itself, can also be very good for business.

The purpose of **Jip**, **Jif** and **Jim** could therefore be two-fold:

* To encourage more humour in the world of business and finance for its own sake.

* To take advantage of the superior business performance that can be expected from companies with a policy of encouraging humour amongst their workers and customers.

As with **ET**, an investor, because the humour fund is based on the FTSE 100 index, could not, in fact, be taking any risk beyond what he is already taking, by having money invested in the stock market. In fact, unless they are already invested in an index fund, they could reduce the risk of their investment under performing the main index by investing in a **JIF**.

The advantages of index funds over conventionally managed funds were spelt out in scene 4 of the previous ACT when the case for **ET** was being made, so we don't need to go over all that again.

For anyone puzzled by the expression 'laughing all the way to the bank', this scene could provide an explanation.

For anyone not convinced of the advantages of humour in business, or indeed any aspect of life, here are one or two interesting facts.

We would like to express our gratitude to Robert Holden, the author of several books on humour, laughing and stress management, for his contribution to putting some 'meat' (apologies vegETarians) on this 'silly' idea.

Humour has all sorts of benefits which human beings are only just beginning to remind themselves of.

1. Top of the list; it makes you happier!

2. Laughing and smiling have been medically proven to boost the immune system of humans.

3. A work environment where people are laughing a lot will suffer lower rates of staff illness than a comparable workplace that lacks humour.

4. A work environment where people are laughing a lot and enjoying themselves will motivate people to actually come to work. (Absenteeism is estimated to cost companies in the UK billions a year. A company encouraging humour at work is likely to suffer significantly lower levels of absenteeism than average.)

5. Humour can reduce stress levels, boost creativity, energy, positive thinking, team spirit, morale and productivity.

6. Perhaps one of the most useful applications of humour for a company is in trying to communicate with its employees and customers. Take this acorn as an example. Could the ideas in it have been communicated more or less effectively without humour? Either way, it certainly makes it more enjoyable to write!

Humour has been widely demonstrated as a method of boosting a listener's or readers interest in the 'message'. Companies encouraging humour in communication are likely to find their message achieving more results than a company happy to bore its workforce to death with whatever crackpot theory management happen to be excited about this week.

Customers are equally receptive to the use of humour. A company successfully using humour in its marketing is likely to outsell its rivals, other things being equal.

We can all vouch personally as to how boring work can be without humour. I am ashamed to say I spent far too long adding to the mountain of extremely unfunny financial research published by City analysts every week. None of the customers of this research are able to read more than a fraction of it, which repeats and duplicates itself anyway, so no-one is actually missing anything by not reading it all.

Books could be filled, and have been filled, detailing the many benefits of humour to us humans, with various tests and research for those people whose sense of humour has become so dormant that they actually need to see evidence of this. Frankly, anybody who needs proof that laughing is good for you is a bit of a lost cause!

Do we all agree that the encouragement of laughter and humour in a workplace could ensure that the company's most important asset, its people, are at their happiest, and therefore their most effective?

If we do accept that humour is a very legitimate and desireable business objective, we need a JOKE INVESTMENT PANEL to ensure that its ranking reflected which companies were most successful in encouraging and utilising humour.

Enter 'The Jip Criteria.'

Obviously, a suitably qualified range of 'experts' would have to be appointed. This could be a panel of well known comics and humorists. Should they ever agree on a criteria for assessing a corporate sense of humour, they would set up a joke index which would rank all the FTSE companies according to how funny they were, in exactly the same way that **ET** and **ESP** could be doing for their criteria.

The criteria could be split 50/50 between a companies **internal** and **external** activities.

For its **external** activities the panel would rate the comic effect of:

a) All TV, Radio, Newspaper and Magazine advertising. This could be done by each company nominating its funniest add in any of those media, and the panel would score each company's nomination, similar to the way the Advertising Industry Awards rate comic adverts.

b) All official literature; sales brochures, manuals, PR releases etc. Again, each company would nominate its funniest item for assessment by **Jip**.

c) The company's Annual Report would be painstakingly searched for any sign of humour. Other comics not serving on the panel would be to hand to provide relief for anyone on the panel overcome with severe frustration.

d) The company's annual meeting would be viewed, either in person or on a video recording, to assess the comic quality of the punchlines delivered by the chairman, or any other humorous, even 'silly', antics performed by other members of the board. The scope here is limitless. King Arthur Costumes and Alien Suits would be viewed with particular favour. The sillier the bETter.

For its **internal** activities the panel would rate the company's commitment to humour by assessing any initiative the company and its employees had instigated that had an element of humour in it.

Robert Holden, in his book, 'Laughter, the Best Medicine', describes 25 possible workplace routes to this goal. Some of which are hilarious!

Without listing them all here, any of those initiatives could be considered evidence of the company's commitment to humour. If you would like your company to get a good score from **JIP**, perhaps a copy of the book could find its way to the MD's desk!

What if companies think **Jip** is a joke?

That could be their loss, and the gain of their rivals who have got the nous, as well as the sense of humour, to realise that humour can actually make a business more successful, *and* profitable.

And since **Jip** could have told **Jim** to buy more of those successful companies shares' for **Jif**, the investors in **Jif** would be able to have a jolly good laugh about the whole thing 'all the way to the bank', which would probably be full of people laughing anyway.

Enter 'The Jip Panel'

These are some preliminary suggestions. They are all people who have demonstrated a comic talent, intentional or otherwise.

John Cleese
Ben Elton
Rick Mayall
Harry Enfield
Urban Warrior
John Four Eyes Egley
Prince Charles
MargarET Thatcher
Neil Kinnock
Alan Clarke
Graham Taylor
Terry Venables
Richard Branson
Jeremy Paxman

How do we get Jim, Jip and Jif off the ground?

Could we have a **Millionaires Laughing Network? MLN. MLN for the Millennium.** Their epoch-making role could be to use their wealth to get the whole world laughing by the year **2000.**

How?

Enter 'The Millionaires' Laughing Network'

Any millionaire or billionaire who serioulsy wants to help launch MLN for the Millenium needs to get serious. This one could be the biggest laugh (and launch) of all time. Laughing is a universal medicine. Jim, with the help of the Millionaires' Laughing Network, could launch a Jif in every stock markET of the world.

Yes. We could have a British **Jif**, an American **Jif**, a Russian **Jif**, a German **Jif**, a Chinese **Jif**, a Japanese **Jif**, an Indian **Jif**, an emerging markets **Jif**, a Multinational **Jif**, a world **Jif**. Has Iraq got a stock market?

Do we need a market research project? No, we will take it on trust that a fund that is going to mirror the main stock markET index but makes people laugh is going to be in demand.

The FTSE Joke Investment Fund is going to be the prototype for the world wide takeover by **JIM** of the world's financial system..

Is this feasible? Could **JIF's** make the leap from concept to reality?

Only one way to find out...

ASK SID WHAT HE THINKS OF **JIM**!

EPILOGUE

A brief Summary of

ENVIRONMENTAL TRACKING CAN INVESTMENT REVOLUTION PREVENT ECOLOGICAL CATASTROPHE

The above text, which is a script for a real life drama, is a humorous description of a very *serious* possibility. The book describes how it might be possible to quite literally trigger an 'environmental revolution' in the world financial markets.

The book asks what is the source of human environmental damage. The answer it finds is the way money is spent and invested. It then demonstrates a very simple and prior to the publication of this book unknown method of harnessing the world's stock markets to the cause of environmental improvement without asking anyone to agree to anything that is not obviously of financial benefit to them, whether they be an investor or a company or a consumer. The book does not content itself with a theoretical approach but, by exploiting the financial knowledge of its author, actually spells out, step by step, how this innovation can be implemented and lead to a transformation of the world's financial and economic system, using the system exactly as it exists. So simple is the essence of the innovation there is no reason why it cannot have made the leap from concept to reality for the beginning of the new millennium.

The book goes on to explain why environmental pricing is the essential linchpin to the solution of the environmental crisis and how the first stock market based solution can create the necessary pressure from business worldwide for the adoption of environmental pricing.

This is a summary of the line of argument the book pursues.

THE PLANET NEEDS A PRACTICAL PLAN TO SAVE THE PlanET
as a matter of *overriding* priority.

MONEY IS POWER
All environmental damage is a consequence of the way money is spent
and invested.

MONEY IS CONCENTRATED IN THE STOCK MarkET
The stock market is owned by millions of small investors with small
investments and a small number of millionaires with large investments.

THE STOCK MARKET NEEDS TO BE GREENED
Then capital can be directed towards desirable green objectives.

SPECIALIST GREEN AND ETHICAL FUNDS DO NOT WORK
They attempt to select a small number of green companies and fail to
create a direct pressure on all companies including the largest who
dominate the economy to improve their environmental performance

WE NEED A GREEN TROJAN HORSE TO ENTER AND
RADICALLY ALTER THE WORLD'S STOCK MARKETS
An investment concept which encourages green behaviour amongst the
largest companies but is safe enough to be welcomed by the majority of
investors who want a return similar to or better than the stock market
index has every chance of succeeding

ET IS AN ABBREVIATION FOR THE **ENVIRONMENTAL
TRACKING CONCEPT**. IT IS BASED ON THE RANKING OF
THE LARGEST COMPANIES IN EACH STOCK MARKET and HAS
BEEN DESIGNED TO BE IMPLEMENTED WORLDWIDE
It requires the establishment of an independent Environmental Scoring
Panel (**ESP**) recruited from across the entire business and
environmental spectrum in each country and specifically including
green pressure groups. The **ESP** then scores the constituents of the
MAIN STOCK MARKET INDEX IN EACH COUNTRY according to
a transparent easily identifiable 10 point criteria. The initial criteira
has been identified and is based on the best current environmental
practice as demonstrated by the greenest thinking companies and the

various official and non governmental bodies involved in raising
environmental standards. The role of the **ESP** is to continue refining
the criteria upwards as the least green catch up and the greenest
become greener.

THE **ET CONCEPT** RE-WEIGHTS THE NORMAL INDEX
ACCORDING TO THE RANKING ESTABLISHED BY THE **ESP**
AND UPDATES THIS RANKING TWICE YEARLY
The combining of a public competitive ranking of the largest
companies in each stock market with an index fund creates an
environmental and financial pressure on each of them that cannot be
ignored. By penalising those companies at the bottom and rewarding
those at the top by altering the supply and demand for the shares of
each company according to its position in the ranking
ET can become a stock market revolution
because the larger ET becomes,
the greater the incentive to climb up the rankings
and the greater the pressure to avoid falling to the bottom.

BECAUSE THIS INVESTMENT METHOD IS SO SIMPLE AND
SAFE THERE IS NO LOGICAL REASON WHY **ET** COULD NOT
EVENTUALLY ACHIEVE ITS TARGET OF MANAGING 50% OF
THE SHARES IN EACH STOCK MARKET AROUND THE WORLD
Since 'Ownership is Control', as Karl Marx aptly put it,
money would be directed according to a green criteria all around the
planet in a very short period of time because, ultimately, the boards of
companies have to carry out the wishes of their shareholders or face
replacement BY A BOARD OF THE SHAREHOLDERS CHOOSING.

THE ONLY LOGICAL REASON **ET** WOULD NOT BE ABLE TO
ACHIEVE THIS TARGET WOULD BE IF THE MAJORITY OF
INVESTORS COULD BE PRESENTED WITH A SUPERIOR
INVESTMENT PROPOSITION
Because the majority of stock market investment is currently invested
in 'managed funds' which in aggregate cannot, by definition,
outperform the index, they represent a level of risk which is
unnecessarily higher than an index based fund. If an environmentally
weighted index fund has been designed to benefit from the
environmental pressures that are appearing in all aspects of business
life and which, on any sane view of the future, must continue to build

up, then that fund must, over time, be able to outperform a conventional index fund.

It therefore presents itself to an investor as the safest stock market investment proposition available. Unless investors can be persuaded to do something that is against both their own financial and environmental interests, this planet is about to experience an **Investment Revolution That Might Prevent Ecological Catastrophe**

**IF YOU WANT TO HELP HERE ARE FIVE THINGS THAT
CAN BE DONE <u>TODAY</u> TO HELP 'ET' MAKE A DIFFERENCE:**

1. **Ask your local School/College/Library to stock a copy of this
   drama.**
2. **Write to leading business and environmental organisations
   urging them to participate in ESP - The Environmental Scoring
   Panel.**

3. **Write to your pension fund trustees/financial advisor/
   stockbroker asking them to participate in ET - The
   Environmental Tracking Concept.**

4. **Send a donation payable to the EIO (ET Campaign Fund) to
   enable it to promote ET and ESP on a worldwide basis either
   by paying direct into:
   Co-op Bank Account No: 70223817
   Or by post to:
   Co-op Bank Business Direct
   Olympic House
   6 Olympic Court
   Montford Street
   Salford M5 2QP**

5. **Finally, don't forget to buy and wear an ET-shirt available
   from 'Millennium Messages on ET-Shirts' P.0. Box 11780
   Greenwich SE7 7ZT. You will be sent a catalogue of wacky T-
   shirt designs and other promotional ideas.**

DO YOUR BIT TO CARRY AN IMPORTANT MESSAGE